LIGHTPLANE OWNER'S MAINTENANCE GUIDE

By Cliff Dossey

MODERN AIRCRAFT SERIES

TAB BOOKS

Blue Ridge Summit, Pa. 17214

FIRST EDITION

FIRST PRINTING—DECEMBER 1977
SECOND PRINTING—JANUARY 1979

Copyright © 1977 by TAB BOOKS

Printed in the United States of America

Library of Congress Cataloging in Publication Data

Chisty, Joe
    Lightplane owner's maintenance guide.

    (Modern aircraft series)
    Includes index.
    1. Airplanes, Private—Maintenance and repair. I. Title.
ISBN 0-8306-9995-3
ISBN 0-8306-2244-6 pbk.

CONTENTS

FOREWORD

The author is much indebted to the anonymous authors of the FAA publications, *A&P Mechanics Airframe Handbook* (EA-AC 65-15), *Aircraft Inspection & Repair* (EA-AC 43.13-1A&2), *A&P Mechanics General Handbook* (EA-AC-65-9), *FAR Handbook for Aviation Mechanics* (EA-AC FAR1), and *A&P Mechanics Power-plant Handbook* (EA-AC 65-12), distributed by the U.S. Government Printing Office, and speedily available from the Aviation Mechanics Foundation, Box 750, Basin, WY 82410.

Also, to Warren and Ruth Spencer, who are unexcelled in the refurbishing of wood and fabric airplanes; to versatile Bill Welch, engineer, author and airplane-fixer; FBO Al Synder, and to the dedicated people at Stits Aircraft, Riverside, CA, for material contained herein, including drawings, advice, and the usual willingness-to-help that invariably characterizes aviation maintenance people.

To all of these, we tip our mechanic's cap in respect and appreciation. Their aid, while in no way constituting an endorsement of this work, was invaluable and, with our own years of experience in this field cranked in, results, we think, in a sound and useful maintenance/repair guide for the pilot-owner.

Cliff Dossey

CHAPTER 1
KEEP IT LEGAL

Federal Aviation Regulations state that "the holder of a pilot certificate issued under FAR 61 may perform preventive maintenance on any aircraft owned or operated by him that is not used in air carrier service." Such preventative maintenance is specifically listed in Part 43, Appendix A, of the FARs:

1. Removal, installation, and repair of landing gear tires.
2. Replacing elastic shock absorber cords on landing gear.
3. Servicing landing gear shock struts by adding oil, air, or both.
4. Servicing landing gear wheel bearings, such as cleaning and greasing.
5. Replacing defective safety wiring or cotter keys.
6. Lubrication not requiring disassembly other than removal of nonstructural items such as cover plates, cowlings, and fairings.
7. Making simple fabric patches not requiring rib stitching or the removal of structural parts or control surfaces.
8. Replenishing hydraulic fluid in the hydraulic reservoir.
9. Refinishing decorative coating of fuselage, wings, tail group surfaces (excluding balanced control surfaces), fairings, cowling, landing gear, cabin, or cockpit interior when removal or disassembly of any primary structure or operating system is not required.
10. Applying preservative or protective material to components where no disassembly of any primary structure or

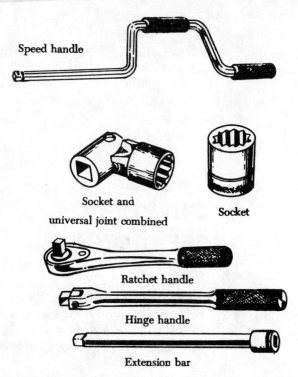

Speed handle

Socket and
universal joint combined

Socket

Ratchet handle

Hinge handle

Extension bar

Among the tools you'll need is a set of 1/4-inch socket wrenches.

operating system is involved and where such coating is not prohibited or is not contrary to good practices.

11. Repairing upholstery and decorative furnishings of the cabin or cockpit interior when the repairing does not require disassembly of any primary structure or operating system or interfere with an operating system or affect primary structure of the aircraft.

12. Making small, simple repairs to fairings, nonstructural cover plates, cowlings, and small patches and reinforcements not changing the contour so as to interfere with proper airflow.

13. Replacing side windows where that work does not interfere with the structure or any operating system such as controls, electrical equipment, etc.

14. Replacing safety belts.

15. Replacing seats or seat parts with replacement parts approved for the aircraft, not involving disassembly of any primary structure or operating system.

16. Troubleshooting and repairing broken circuits in landing light wiring circuits.
17. Replacing bulbs, reflectors, and lenses of position and landing lights.
18. Replacing wheels or skis where no weight and balance computation is involved.
19. Replacing any cowling not requiring removal of the propeller or disconnection of flight controls.
20. Replacing or cleaning spark plugs and setting of spark plug gap clearance.
21. Replacing any hose connection except hydraulic connections.
22. Replacing prefabricated fuel lines.
23. Cleaning fuel and oil strainers.
24. Replacing batteries and checking fluid level and specific gravity.

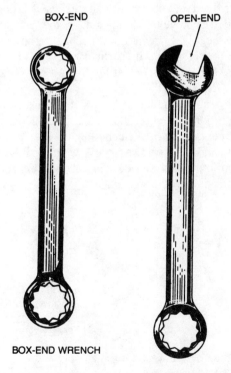

BOX-END

OPEN-END

BOX-END WRENCH

COMBINATION WRENCH

Also needed are open-end wrenches, 3/8-inch through 3/4-inch in size.

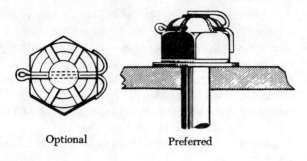

Optional   Preferred

Cotter pin installation.

25. Removing and installing glider wings and tail surfaces that are specifically designed for quick removal and installation and when such removal and installation can be accomplished by the pilot.

You may go beyond the above listed operations *only* if you are working under the direct supervision of a licensed aircraft mechanic (A&P). There are, however, limitations to the airframe and powerplant ratings held by many aircraft mechanics, and major repairs (or even lesser repairs in which a particular A&P has had no previous experience; FAR Part 65:81) must be "signed off" by an A&P with an Inspector's Rating (AI).

It isn't advisable to fudge on any of this because maintenance and repair operations are entered in the airplane's logs and the logs are legal documents. The FAA can be mighty displeased with false entries therein, and has the power to levy what the FAA regards as a penalty appropriate to the seriousness of the offense—up to and including suspension of one's certificate.

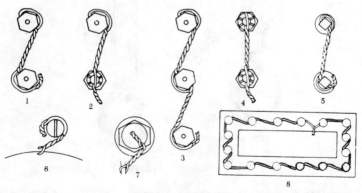

Safety wiring methods.

There is, of course, a more compelling reason for keeping it legal: Your own safety. That's what the FARs are all about.

Before we take up a detailed discussion of the above-listed operations, let's consider your minimum tool needs and the necessity of maintaining good relations with your local A&P.

Over a given period of time, you are going to need advice on a number of things from your A&P, so don't bug him unnecessarily. Don't ask to borrow his tools, especially the expensive ones. Don't ask him to halt work on someone else's airplane (for which he's being paid) to provide you with a cotter key or "a little dab of grease." He's

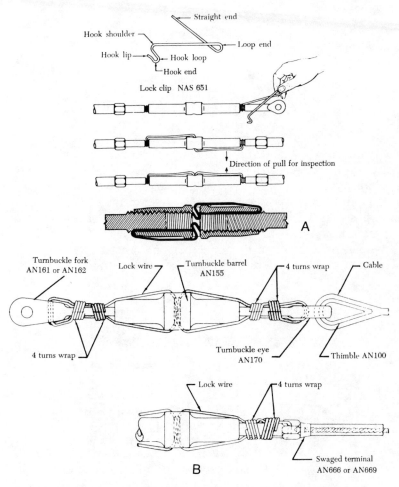

Safetying turnbuckles; A) Clip-locking method; B) Wire-wrapping.

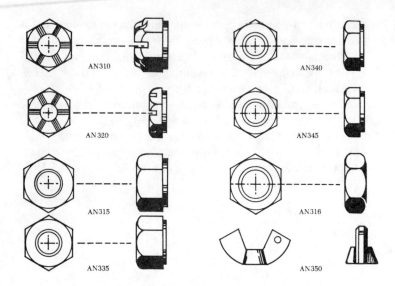

AN310

AN320

AN315

AN335

AN340

AN345

AN316

AN350

Types of non-selflocking aircraft nuts.

already got one or two other such "customers" on the airport, and chances are they have already used up much of his forbearance.

On the other hand, any A&P worth his ratings is sincerely interested in promoting good maintenance practices, and most will agree that owner-maintenance, to the extent that it is practical and legal, serves this goal. If you inspect, and at least partially maintain your own airplane, you will *know* your airplane; you will understand its operating systems, and you will sometimes spot a developing or incipient problem before it becomes a problem—and before its

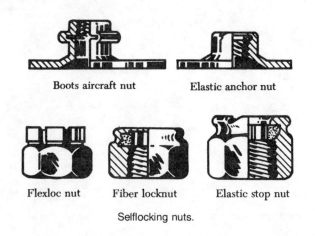

Boots aircraft nut   Elastic anchor nut

Flexloc nut   Fiber locknut   Elastic stop nut

Selflocking nuts.

12

remedy becomes expensive. And such intimacy with your machine incvitably adds to your proficiency as a pilot.

Now, about those tools:

1. If your airplane is a tri-gear with conventional elevators and horizontal stabilizer, you'll need four small sandbags in your T-hangar which you'll use to lift the nose-wheel for servicing. Place the sandbags on the stabilizer, two to a side, close to the fuselage.

We don't recommend this procedure on planes with stabilators. To service Cherokee nose-wheels, we use a three-foot length of 4×4 (or 2×6), with a piece of carpeting on one side, which is placed beneath the first bulkhead. The Cherokee belly is heavily ribbed and easily accommodates this load.

Mooneys, which employ rubber biscuits in compression, will accept a bar through the housing to provide a jack point. Other light aircraft either have jack pads or may be jacked up with the aid of simple jack attachments (see accompanying illustration).

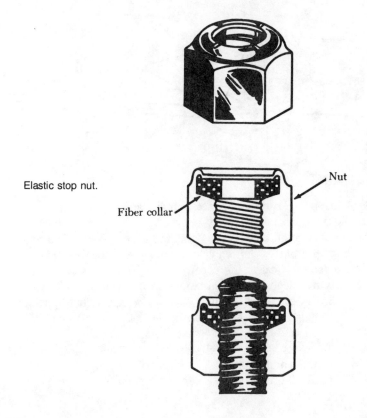

Elastic stop nut.

Nut

Fiber collar

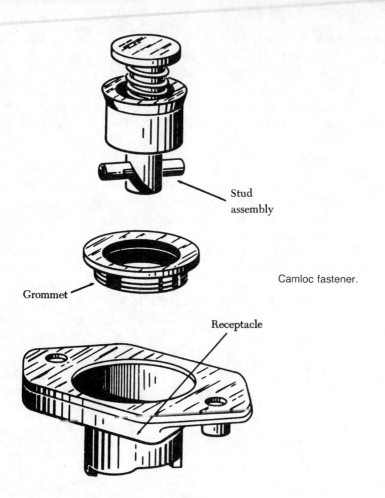

Stud
assembly

Grommet

Camloc fastener.

Receptacle

In any case, always refer to your airplane's maintenance manual for instructions on jacking up your machine. A lot of personal injury, as well as aircraft damage, has resulted from makeshift methods of jacking up airplanes. Automobile bumper jacks should *never* be used. The most practical is the screw-type scissors jack. A 1-1/2-ton capacity hydraulic jack would be our second choice.

2. Six pieces of two-inch angle-iron, each about four inches long, to be used as wheel chocks. These won't slide on concrete.

3. A five-gallon can of solvent; dish pan, rags, and parts-washing brush.

4. Small grease gun for zerk fittings on retractable-gear aircraft.

5. Oil squirt can.
6. One-lb can wheel bearing grease, heavy, fibrous type (do not use wheel bearing grease made for late model automobiles).
7. Quart can of hydraulic brake fluid; make sure it is the kind recommended for your aircraft.
8. Tire pressure gauge.
9. Portable air tank with hose.
10. Soft-faced hammer.
11. Common pliers, duckbill pliers, and diagonals ("dikes").
12. Phillips screwdriver and several common screwdrivers in various lengths, four to 12 inches.

Installed fastener

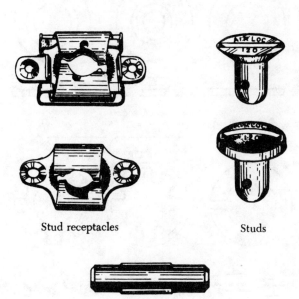

Stud receptacles

Studs

Cross pin

Airloc fastener.

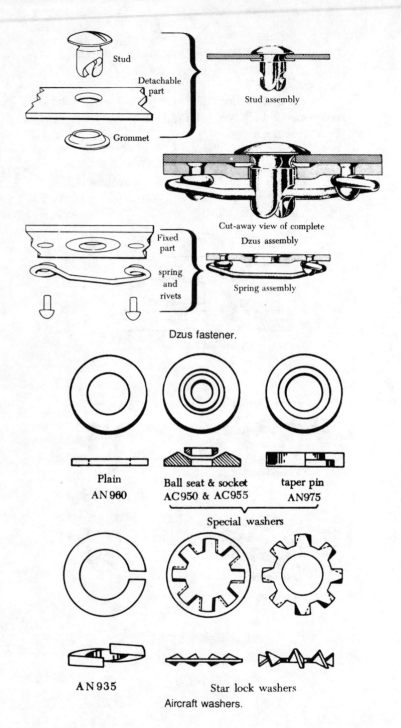

Stud

Detachable part

Grommet

Stud assembly

Cut-away view of complete
Dzus assembly

Fixed part

spring
and
rivets

Spring assembly

Dzus fastener.

Plain
AN 960

Ball seat & socket
AC950 & AC955

taper pin
AN975

Special washers

AN 935

Star lock washers

Aircraft washers.

16

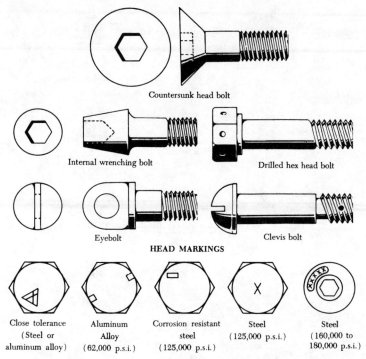

Countersunk head bolt

Internal wrenching bolt

Drilled hex head bolt

Eyebolt

Clevis bolt

HEAD MARKINGS

Close tolerance
(Steel or
aluminum alloy)

Aluminum
Alloy
(62,000 p.s.i.)

Corrosion resistant
steel
(125,000 p.s.i.)

Steel
(125,000 p.s.i.)

Steel
(160,000 to
180,000 p.s.i.)

Aircraft bolts and bolthead markings.

13. 1/4-inch socket set with ratchet and extension drives.
14. Set of open-end wrenches, 3/8 through 3/4-inch.
15. Spark plug socket wrench, 7/8-inch.
16. Take an empty cigar box (or similar container) to your A&P and ask him to sell you a selection of sheet metal screws, aircraft bolts, nuts, and washers, along with a length of safety wire and cotter keys. This will not only make things handier for you later on, but demonstrates your consideration for your mechanic while letting him know that you're

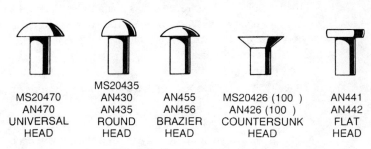

MS20470
AN470
UNIVERSAL
HEAD

MS20435
AN430
AN435
ROUND
HEAD

AN455
AN456
BRAZIER
HEAD

MS20426 (100)
AN426 (100)
COUNTERSUNK
HEAD

AN441
AN442
FLAT
HEAD

Aircraft rivets and code numbers.

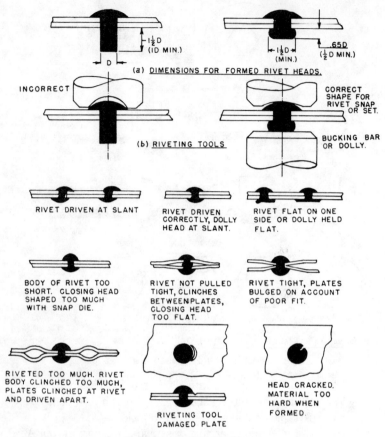

(a) DIMENSIONS FOR FORMED RIVET HEADS.

(b) RIVETING TOOLS

INCORRECT

CORRECT SHAPE FOR RIVET SNAP OR SET.

BUCKING BAR OR DOLLY.

RIVET DRIVEN AT SLANT

RIVET DRIVEN CORRECTLY, DOLLY HEAD AT SLANT.

RIVET FLAT ON ONE SIDE OR DOLLY HELD FLAT.

BODY OF RIVET TOO SHORT. CLOSING HEAD SHAPED TOO MUCH WITH SNAP DIE.

RIVET NOT PULLED TIGHT, CLINCHES BETWEEN PLATES, CLOSING HEAD TOO FLAT.

RIVET TIGHT, PLATES BULGED ON ACCOUNT OF POOR FIT.

RIVETED TOO MUCH. RIVET BODY CLINCHED TOO MUCH, PLATES CLINCHED AT RIVET AND DRIVEN APART.

RIVETING TOOL DAMAGED PLATE

HEAD CRACKED. MATERIAL TOO HARD WHEN FORMED.

(C) RIVET IMPERFECTIONS.

Riveting practice and rivet imperfections.

not there to mooch. We really can't say too much on this subject. You are going to need your A&P's professional advice—and services—from time to time, and when you do, the respect you've offered him is going to be returned.

17. The maintenance and parts manuals for your aircraft. Always check your maintenance manual for special instructions prior to each maintenance operation.

18. A good droplight with cord at least 15 feet in length.

19. A small mirror for inspecting hard-to-get-at places. An angled dentist's mirror is handy.

20. Valve core extractor.

You'll need one additional item: Plenty of time to perform each maintenance operation. Don't rush!

CHAPTER 2
TIRES, WHEEL
BEARINGS, & SHOCK STRUTS

First, let us clearly state that, even if you are able to borrow aircraft tripod wing-jacks, and are determined to jack up the entire airplane for whatever purpose, you are living dangerously. This is a job for your A&P to handle. As pilot-owner, you should limit yourself to jacking up one wheel at a time. Airplanes are balanced machines, and lifting them from their normal three-point ground stance can be tricky. Tips from the FAAs *A&P Mechanic's General Handbook* underscore some the problems:

"Since jacking procedures and safety precautions vary for different types of aircraft, consult the applicable aircraft manufacturer's maintenance instructions for specific jacking instructions.

"...before raising an aircraft on jacks, all workstands and other equipment should be removed from under and near the aircraft. No one should remain in the aircraft while it is being raised or lowered, unless maintenance manual procedures require such practice for observing leveling instruments in the aircraft.

"The aircraft must be located in a level position, well protected from the wind. A hangar should be used if possible. The manufacturer's maintenance instructions should be consulted for the location of the jacking points. These jacking points are usually located in relation to the aircraft center of gravity so the plane will be well balanced on the jacks. However, there are some exceptions to this. On some aircraft it may be necessary to add weight to the nose or tail to achieve a safe balance. Sandbags are usually used for this purpose.

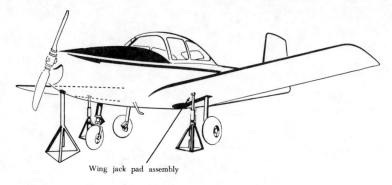

Wing jack pad assembly

Jacking a complete aircraft.

"...prior to jacking the aircraft, an overall survey of the complete situation should be made to determine if any hazards to the aircraft or personnel exist. Tripod jacks of the appropriate size for the aircraft should be placed under the aircraft jacking points and perfectly centered to prevent them from cocking when the aircraft is raised. The legs of the jacks should be checked to see that they will not interfere with the operation to be performed.

"At least three points are provided on the aircraft for jacking purposes; a fourth place on some aircraft is used to stabilize the aircraft while it is being jacked....

"Most aircraft have jack pads at the jack points. Others have removable jack pads that are inserted into receptacles bolted into place prior to the jacking. The correct jack pad should be used in all cases. The function of the jack pad is to ensure that the aircraft load is properly distributed at the jack point and to provide a convex bearing surface to mate with the concave jack stem.

"Prior to jacking, determine if the aircraft configuration will permit jacking. There may be equipment or fuel which has to be removed if serious structural damage is to be avoided during jacking. If any other work is in progress on the aircraft, ascertain if any critical panels have been removed. On some aircraft the stress panels or plates must be in place when the aircraft is jacked to avoid structural damage.

"Extend the jacks until they contact the jack pads. A final check for alignment of the jacks should be made before the aircraft is raised, since most accidents during jacking are the result of misaligned jacks.

"When the aircraft is ready to be raised, a man should be stationed at each jack. The jacks should be operated simultaneously to keep the aircraft as level as possible and to avoid overloading of any of the jacks. This can be accomplished by having the crew leader stand in front of the aircraft and give instructions to the men operating the jacks. Caution should be observed, since on many jacks the piston can be raised beyond the safety point; therefore, never raise an aircraft any higher than is necessary to accomplish the job.

"This area around the aircraft should be secured while the aircraft is on jacks. Climbing on the aircraft should be held to an absolute minimum, and no violent movements should be made by persons who are required to go aboard. Any cradles or necessary supports should be placed under the fuselage or wings at the earliest possible time, particularly if the aircraft is to remain jacked up for any length of time.

"Before releasing jack pressure and lowering the aircraft, make certain that all cribbing, workstands, equipment, and people are clear of the airplane, that the landing gear is down and locked, and that all ground locking devices are properly installed."

Jacking One Wheel of an Aircraft

We have already mentioned the use of sandbags on the horizontal stabilizer to lift the nose wheel of some tri-gear aircraft. On

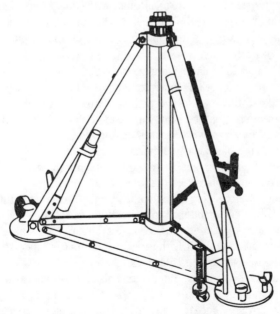

Typical tripod aircraft jack.

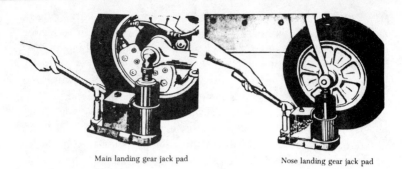

Main landing gear jack pad   Nose landing gear jack pad

Jacking one wheel.

others a low, single-base jack is used. Whatever the method, you will, of course, chock the main landing gear wheels fore and aft to prevent movement of the airplane. If your plane is a "tail-dragger," the tailwheel must be locked.

Whether jacking the nose wheel or one of the mains, raise it only as high as necessary to clear the concrete surface.

Tires and Wheels

To remove a wheel for tire repair/replacement and/or bearing lubrication, first check your maintenance manual for special instructions. Also heed what the manual has to say about removing the brakes, although this is a simple operation on most light aircraft.

Take out the valve core to make sure that the tire is completely deflated. Most lightplane wheels are made in two halves, bolted together. You risk serious injury, and destruction of the wheel, if you remove these bolts while the tire is inflated. Also, break the tire bead from the rim before removing these bolts. To break the bead, we use a 12-inch screwdriver with its end filed to a rounded shape.

Next, take out the wheel bolts and then lift out the rear half of the wheel. This minimizes the risk of damaging the valve stem with removal of the front half of the wheel.

Inner tube patching is the same as with automobile tubes; but the most common cause of airplane tube/tire (including tubeless type tires) leaks is damage to the valve stem or near its base. This is often traceable to contact with the wheel pants (or "speed fairings," as airplane salesmen like to call them).

Take the bearings and bearing seals (felt retainers) out of the wheel and clean with solvent. Check bearing condition. If any rollers fall from the roller cage, or if any rollers or the roller race are scored or pitted, the bearing must be replaced. Dry the bearing and repack, by hand, with wheel bearing grease, working it into the bearing assembly with your fingertips.

Carefully inspect the wheel while it is disassembled, and thoroughly clean if corrosion is present. Smooth and repaint bare corroded spots with a protective coating such as zinc chromate primer and aluminum lacquer or some other equally effective coating to prevent further corrosion. Replace wheels having severe corrosion which might affect their strength.

Also replace wheels which wobble excessively due to deformation resulting from a severe side-load impact. In questionable cases, consult your A&P. Rim areas require special attention because this is where most dents and cracks appear.

In split-type wheels, the bolt holes will become elongated if not properly tightened. Such damage can be repaired by the use of inserts. Any movement between the wheel halves will cause elongation of the bolt holes, and if the wear is too great to be corrected with inserts, the wheel will have to be scrapped.

Carefully inspect wheels used with tubeless tires for damage to the wheel flange and for proper sealing of the valve.

The bearing seals (felt retainers) should be maintained in a soft, absorbent condition. If these become hardened, wash in solvent, and if this fails to soften them, they should be replaced.

We should mention that the wheel bearings should be serviced every six months or every 100 hours, whichever comes first.

When remounting the tire, remember that aircraft tires have balancing marks. On some brands the red dot is lined up with the valve stem; on others it is opposite the valve stem. So check this with your tire dealer when installing new tires.

Before placing the tire on the wheel, however, you should inflate the tube inside the tire to insure that it is well seated and free of wrinkles; then leave just enough air in the tube to allow it to hold its shape. And it is probably best to reinstall the bearings in the wheel halves before mounting the tire, because this allows you to clean away excess grease. An excessive amount of grease in the wheel bearings will be thrown by centrifugal force through the split wheel to reach the inner tube. Oil and grease deteriorate tires and tubes.

Rather than remount the tire on the wheel, it is probably more accurate to say that you install the wheel halves on the tire, beginning with the wheel half containing the valve hole. Then, turn it over and install the rear half of the wheel.

Now, most aircraft wheels are not marked for any particular mating of the two halves, but a few are; so check the wheel halves to see if there are marks indicating that they must be lined up a certain way. As you put the two wheel halves together, make sure that you do not pinch the inner tube (if the tube is inflated enough to hold its shape, this danger is minimized).

Next, put the bolts back in the wheel disc and tighten to the torque value recommended in your airplane's maintenance manual. The wheel bolts should have washers under the nut-side, and most wheels also have washers under the head-side of each bolt. Self-locking nuts should be replaced if the inserts are worn enough to allow you to screw them on with your fingers.

After the wheel has been reassembled and the bolts properly torqued, and before reinstalling the valve core in the valve stem, inflate then deflate the tire to make sure that it is seated as it should be and that the bead is evenly aligned around its circumference. Then, return the valve core to the valve stem and inflate to recommended pressure.

Replacing the wheel on the axle, tighten the axle-nut just enough to produce a slight drag, then back it off approximately 1/2 turn. The axle-nut should be tight enough to prevent any side-play of the wheel, but should not induce any pre-load. Use a *new* cotter key, and make sure that it is tight and that the sharp ends are so positioned that they cannot damage a bearing seal. Check the wheel-pants mounts for cracks before reinstalling them.

We should mention that wheel pants can hide tire defects, especially cuts in the tread, or flat spots caused by an out-of-balance tire. With part of the tire resting on the pavement, and most of the rest of it covered by the pant, it's easy to unknowingly allow tire damage to develop to the point of failure, while that part of the tire you can see may look very good indeed.

It's always best to let your airplane sit overnight after repairing or replacing a tire. Then, if you have a leak, the tire will go flat in the hangar rather than in the air.

Shock Struts

A typical pneumatic/hydraulic shock strut uses compressed air combined with hydraulic fluid to absorb shock loads, and is usually referred to as the air/oil or oleo strut.

A shock strut is made up essentially of two telescoping cylinders or tubes, with externally closed ends. These comprise the cylinder and piston, forming an upper and lower chamber for movement of the fluid. The lower chamber is always filled with fluid, while the upper chamber contains compresses air. An orifice between the chambers provides a passage for the fluid into the upper chamber during compression of the strut, and a return during extension of the strut.

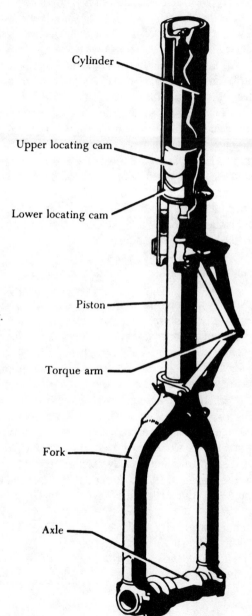

Cylinder

Upper locating cam

Lower locating cam

Piston

Nose gear shock strut.

Torque arm

Fork

Axle

Most shock struts employ a metering pin to control the rate of fluid flow into the upper chamber. On some types of shock struts, a metering tube is used instead of a variable-shaped pin, but strut operation is the same.

Some shock struts are equipped with a damping or snubbing device consisting of a recoil valve on the piston to reduce the rebound during the extension stroke.

A fitting consisting of a fluid filler inlet and air valve assembly is located near the upper end of each shock strut to provide a means of filling the strut with hydraulic fluid and inflating it with air.

A packing gland designed to seal the sliding joint between the upper and lower telescoping cylinders is installed in the open end of the outer cylinder. A packing gland wiper ring is also installed in a groove in the lower bearing or gland nut on most shock struts to keep the sliding surface of the piston free from dirt, ice, snow, etc.

The majority of shock struts are equipped with torque arms attached to the cylinder and piston to maintain correct alignment of the wheel. Those shock struts without torque arms have splined piston heads and cylinders.

Nose gear shock struts are provided with an upper locating cam attached to the upper cylinder and a mating lower locating cam attached to the piston. These cams line up the wheel and axle assembly in the straight-ahead position when the shock strut is fully extended. This prevents the nosewheel from being cocked to one side when the nose gear is retracted, thus guarding against possible damage to the aircraft structure. These cams also keep the nosewheel in a straight-ahead position prior to landing. Some nosewheel shock struts are fitted with shimmy dampers.

All shock struts are provided with an instruction plate or decal which gives directions for filling the strut with fluid and for inflating the strut with air. But many of these disappear with time, and in any case it's always best to refer to your airplane's maintenance manual.

The strut must be fully deflated to add oil, and you will jack the aircraft and allow the strut to be fully extended before deflating it. If you deflate the strut while it is compressed, a geyser of oil will blow out through the valve. Also, extended or not, keep your face away from the strut valve while deflating it. That's high-pressure air, and it can be dangerous to your eyes.

It should be noted that, although the strut valve core may greatly resemble the valve cores in your tires, they are not the same. The valve core in the shock strut has neoprene seals, which are impervious to deterioration from oil.

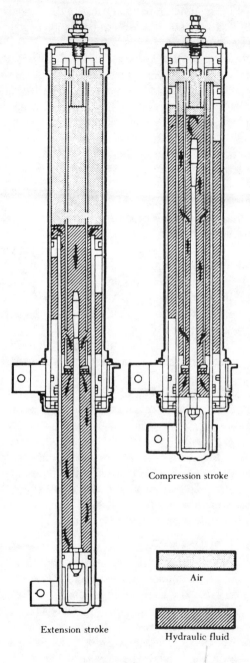

Air

Hydraulic fluid

Extension stroke

Compression stroke

Shock strut operation.

27

We don't recommend that you remove the core from the strut valve to deflate, but instead control the deflation by releasing the air pressure slowly.

With the shock strut fully extended and deflated, attach a length of plastic hose (the kind your doctor uses on intravenous bottles works nicely) to the valve and immerse the opposite end of the hose in your can of hydraulic strut oil. Then, by alternately compressing and extending the strut by hand, simply pump in the fluid to the proper level.

If the strut won't pump fluid, it needs new seals.

This method will work equally well in adding fluid to the main wheel shock struts. Keep in mind, however, that while the normal air pressure in most lightplane nosewheel struts is less then 100 lbs/sq in. the main wheel struts may carry up to 500 lbs/sq in. pressure, which is why a strut pump or other source of clean, high-pressure air is needed to inflate main gear struts when they are compressed with the weight of the airplane.

However, since there is relatively little air in a shock strut, the 100 lbs or so pressure that your portable air tank will handle may be sufficient if you inflate the main gear strut while the wheel is jacked and the strut fully extended.

While the airplane is jacked, check the bolts and connections on the strut's scissors arms for looseness. This is the source of a lot of vibration.

Some older aircraft, such as the Aeronca, have all oil in the shock struts; no air. Make certain that you service with the proper type of oil.

If your airplane is equipped with rubber shock cord rings, we strongly recommend that you have these replaced by your A&P when the time comes. True, FARs define this operation as "preventive maintenance," and it's legal for you to do it yourself. But special tools are required; it's easy to damage the new rings during installation, and this is a task that can be dangerous.

Cleaning & Lubricating

You should use only easily removable neutral solutions when cleaning landing gear components. Any advantage, such as speed or effectiveness, gained by using cleaners containing corrosive materials, may be quickly counteracted if these fluids become trapped in close-fitting surfaces and crevices. Wear points, such as landing gear up-and-down latches, jack screws, door hinges, pulleys, cables, bellcranks, and all pressure-type grease fittings (zerks) should be relubricated after every cleaning operation.

During winter operation, excess grease may congeal and cause increased loads on gear retraction system electric motors and hydraulic pumps. This can lead to component malfunctions. Therefore, stress cleanliness during and after lubrication.

Emergency Systems

Exercise the emergency landing gear system periodically to insure proper operation and to prevent inactivity, dirt, and corrosion from rendering the system inoperative in case it is needed. Check for proper safetying of triggering mechanisms, and for the presence of required placards and any necessary accessories. This of course requires that the aircraft be jacked, which in turn means that you must carefully follow your maintenance manual's jacking instructions and work with experienced help, or consign this job to your A&P.

CHAPTER 3

FABRIC—COTTON AND LINEN

There are several kinds of fabric in use for the covering of aircraft structures which are approved by the FAA: The venerable Grade A cotton, Irish linen, and the newer synthetics which are marketed under various trade names, but all of which are polyesters of the "Dacron" type. There are also some fiberglass coverings around (Razorback).

Most older "ragwings" will be covered with Grade A cotton or Irish linen. Later model production craft, such as the Champion Citabria, will be covered with one of the new synthetics.

Generally speaking, Grade A cotton, properly finished and well maintained, will last six to eight years if the airplane is kept hangared (sun is fabric's worst enemy; which is why the upper wing surfaces usually go first). Irish linen will last up to twice as long as cotton when properly cared for. And, although the makers of the new synthetics claim that these fabrics will last for the life of the airplane, this is really a moot point, because the internal structure will have to be refurbished after ten to 15 years of average use. Some wood will have to be cleaned of oil or revarnished; 4130 steel tubing will have accumulated some rust, and aluminum members will show some corrosion.

This structural refurbishing is especially necessary to wood-framed wings, because moisture can collect under the metal fittings and deterioration of the wood can set in without the damage being apparent unless the wing covering is off and the fittings removed.

Also, such fittings should be inspected under a magnifying glass for hairline cracks that may not admit to discovery if the wing is covered.

Most synthetic fabric covers are heavier than cotton or linen because most require more filler for a comparable finish. However, the synthetics do maintain high tensile strengths indefinitely, and will probably last as long as you want them to. These include such trade names as Ceconite, Dacron, and Stits Poly-Fiber. There are others.

Grade A cotton fabric must test (tensile) new, at minimum 80 lb strength, warp and fill (both directions). When the test strength is down to 56 lbs, it must be replaced. This is the standard for airplanes with placarded do-not-exceed airspeeds of 150 mph. Irish linen, several years old, will often test above 80 lbs; and the synthetics are all well above this minimum, apparently for "life." The Stits Poly-Fiber, for example, is offered in two weights. The 3.7 oz per sq yd cloth tests 130 lbs per sq in., while the 2.7 oz per sq yard has an average strength of 95 lbs per inch width.

When covering a complete aircraft, procedures are practically the same for cotton, linen, and the synthetics; but tautening and finishing procedures are different, and therefore repair and patching

Aircraft dope and fabric experts were plentiful 50 years ago. View of the WACO factory above shows WACO 10s under construction in 1927 at Troy, Ohio. Engines are the fames OX-5s of 90-hp, a water-cooled V-8.

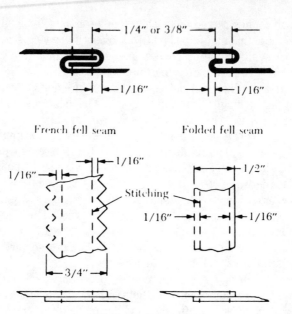

Machine-sewed seams.

requires that you identify the finish, because the butyrate dopes used on most cotton and linen fabrics may not properly bond to a synthetic fabric finished with Poly Tone or other special finish.

Repair of Tears in Fabric

Repair tears by sewing the torn edges together using a baseball stitch and doping a piece of pinked-edge fabric over the tear. If the tear is a straight rip, the sewing is started at one end so that, as the seam is made, the edges will be drawn tightly together throughout its entire length. For a right-angled tear, start the sewing at the corner or point so that the edges of the cover will be held in place while the seams are being made.

The sewing is done with a curved needle and well-waxed thread. Clean the surface to be covered by the patch by rubbing the surface with a rag dipped in dope, wiping dry with a clean rag, or by scraping the surface with a putty knife after it has been softened with fresh dope. Dope solvent or acetone may be used for the same purpose, but care should be taken that it does not drop through on the inside of the opposite surface, causing the dope to blister. Cut a patch of sufficient size from airplane cloth to cover the tear and extend at least 1-1/2 inches beyond the tear in all directions. The

32

edges of the patch should either be pinked similar to surface tape, or frayed out about 1/4 inch on all edges.

Doped-On Patches

Unsewed (doped-on) repairs may be made on all aircraft fabric-covered surfaces provided the never-exceed speed is not greater than 150 mph, and if the damage does not exceed 16 inches in any direction. Cut out the damaged section making a round or oval shaped opening, trimmed to a smooth contour. Clean the edges of the opening which are to be covered by the patch with a grease solvent. Sand or wash off the dope from the area around the patch with dope thinner. Support the fabric from underneath while sanding.

For holes up to eight inches in size, make the fabric patch of sufficient size to give a lap of at least two inches around the hole. On holes over eight inches in size, make the overlap of the fabric around the hole at least one-quarter of the hole diameter with a maximum limit of lap of four inches. If the hole extends over a wing rib or closer than the required overlap to a rib or other laced member, extend the

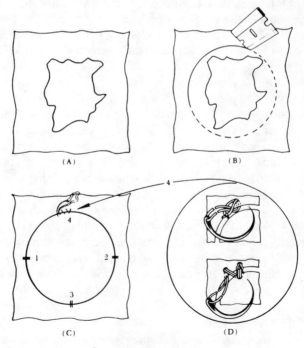

Sewed patch repair.

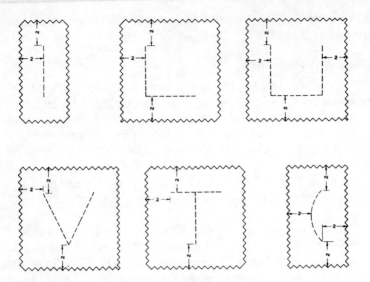

Patching over tears. Dash line represents a stitched tear.

patch at least three inches beyond the rib. In this case, after the edges of the patch have been doped in place and the dope is dried, lace the patch to the rib over a new section of reinforcing tape. Do not remove the old lacing and reinforcing tape. All patches should have pinked edges or, if smooth, should be finished with pinked-edge surface tape.

Now, the FARs do not specifically define the "simple fabric patches" that the pilot-owner is legally allowed to make, except to say that such patches "may not include rib stitching or the removal of structural parts or control surfaces." Therefore, the patch described immediately above would have to be made under the direct supervision of a licensed A&P to keep it legal since it included rib stitching. Whether or not certain other patches may be of the "simple" variety will clearly be a matter of judgment (yours, presumably), because it might be possible to re-cover half a fuselage and call it a simple patch. Still, most things to do with flying demand that you make sound judgments—a number of them in an average cross-country flight— so, sometimes, your common sense obviously is expected to determine the difference between a "simple fabric patch" and one that is best left to your A&P.

Major Re-Covering

Since the re-covering of an entire aircraft is expensive—at least $2,000 currently—and since so few shops willing to do such work will do it right, it's entirely possible that you may decide to re-cover your ragwing yourself and save up to 70% of the cost, while insuring a first class job. You will, of course, pay your A&P to directly supervise your work. The FARs require this—and so does common sense.

One of the most important items in covering aircraft is proper preparation of the structure. Dopeproofing, covering edges which are likely to wear the fabric, preparation of plywood surfaces, and similar operations, if properly done, will do much toward insuring an attractive and long-lasting job.

Treat all parts of the structure which come in contact with doped fabric with a protective coating such as aluminum foil, dope-proof paint, or cellulose tape. Clad aluminum and stainless steel need not be dopeproofed.

Before covering, you must also thoroughly inspect the airframe for any cracks or bends. Check for loose bolts, screws, rivets, and elongated bolt holes at attachments of wings, landing gear, tail surfaces, engine mounts, struts, etc. Look for worn bushings and bearings, and inspect control cables, control cable fairleads and pulleys, along with the proper safetying of bolts and turnbuckle ends. Any wood must be cleaned of oil or grease and revarnished if needed, and metal chromated. In any event, an A&P with an inspector's rating must approve the structure for covering before any covering goes on. If you've missed anything, he'll let you know.

Covering Methods

There are two methods of applying cotton and linen fabric to aircraft structures; the "envelope," which is required for airplanes

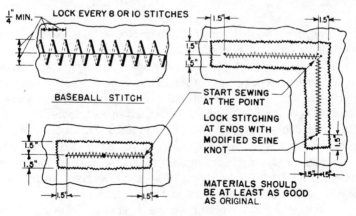

Stitching of tears in fabric.

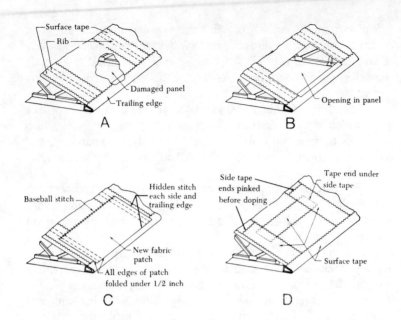

Patching damaged fabric near wing trailing-edge.

with never-exceed speeds of 150 mph or more, and the "blanket" method, normally used on planes that have maximum speeds below 150 mph.

With the envelope method all seams must be machine-sewed with open ends hand-stitched. Pre-sewn envelope kits are available for most airplanes, and these do make things a lot easier. The envelope method normally results in a better finish because the fabric tautens more uniformly since it is in one piece and attached to the airframe only at terminal edges.

With the blanket method, the fabric goes on in pieces, with overlapping edges cemented to the structure.

Most of the synthetics do not employ sewn seams or sewn edges. Each must be put on the airframe in accordance with methods approved by the FAA, and each jobber will include these instructions when he sells the fabric and its associated thread, tapes, cement, thinner, and finishing products. The synthetics, however, aren't all that complicated to work with. A principal difference is that the synthetics are tautened with an electric iron, while linen and cotton are tautened by wetting with distilled water. Fiberglass, by the way, tautens with neither; it remains just as you fit it.

Save the old cover, because it can be very useful as a guide to stitch patterns, locating inspection holes, etc.

If you are using the blanket method (or "cut and lap" method, as it is sometimes called), your fabric will go on the fuselage in four main pieces; one to each side (do the sides first), plus the top and bottom. With the fuselage on its side on sawhorses, drape a piece of fabric over it and plan the cutting with the fabric weave parallel to the line of thrust. The fuselage is the hardest to fit because of its many curves, so take your time and slide the fabric around to get it the way you want it, holding it in place with wooden clothespins.

Allow enough overlap all around so that you can cement the fabric (using fabric cement or nitrate dope) to the *insides* of the top and bottom longerons. This will allow the fabric to later tauten evenly over the visible, outside corners, and makes for a neater job. Use a pencil to mark cutting lines, because ballpoint pens and other markers will bleed through the finish. You can cement each side into place as you cut it, or you can cut all the pieces and then apply them to the structure at one time.

The top and bottom pieces will overlap the side pieces by approximately 1 1/2 inches onto the side panels; and although you may use fabric cement to attach fabric to the inside surfaces of the fuselage tubing or other structural parts, you must use dope to join fabric-to-fabric edges. However, apply only enough dope to cover the overlap area, because the wetting treatment to follow will not tauten doped areas (later application of dope will). Caution: Spread newspapers inside the fuselage to prevent dope from dripping onto the inside surfaces of fabric already in place. Don't pull the fabric tight when cementing it to the structure or the tautening process later will make it over-tight and pull stress-wrinkles from the corners. Sure, it looks baggy at this point, but the wetting process will shrink it amazingly.

If you are making an envelope cover, the pieces of fabric will be held in place with clothespins, and the seams to be sewed pinned, using T-pins spaced about three or four inches apart. Bring the edges together *outward*.

Next, mark along the seam lines on both pieces of fabric, and include any necessary cutouts such as landing gear and strut fittings. Cut away excess fabric, leaving about 5/8-inch allowance from the seam lines. Leave about one-inch allowances at the tailpost, firewall, and around fittings. Then, carefully work the pinned envelope off the rear of the fuselage and have it sewed by someone familiar with sewing machines. A number 16 needle will be required, and aircraft thread, which comes on large spools for commercial machines, will have to be wound onto a smaller spool for use in a home-type machine. The bobbin will also have to be wound.

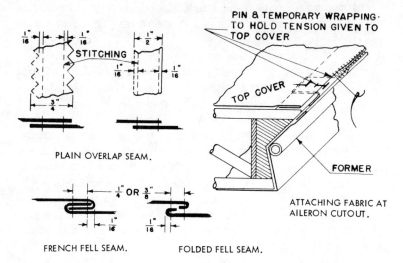

PLAIN OVERLAP SEAM.

FRENCH FELL SEAM. FOLDED FELL SEAM.

ATTACHING FABRIC AT AILERON CUTOUT.

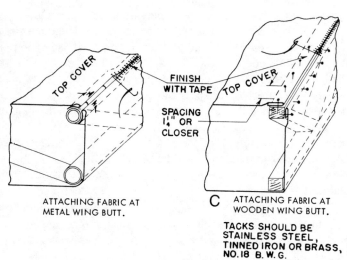

ATTACHING FABRIC AT METAL WING BUTT.

C ATTACHING FABRIC AT WOODEN WING BUTT.

TACKS SHOULD BE STAINLESS STEEL, TINNED IRON OR BRASS, NO.18 B.W.G.

Typical methods of attaching fabric.

The sewing should be done slightly to the outside of the pencilled lines; and you may leave one of the side-to-bottom seams unsewn and, with pins removed (the seam is marked with pencil on both pieces), slip the cover back onto the fuselage to make sure you have a proper fit. If necessary, the unsewn seam may be re-marked a little to the inside or outside to achieve a better fit. Because of the doubled fabric at the seams, the envelope may fit slightly tighter than you expected.

After stitching, and while the envelope is still wrong-side out, iron the seam edges so that they will lie smoothly along the longerons. Wrinkles or sharp folds in the cloth, especially linen, should also be ironed out—but do *not* wet or dampen the fabric.

Return the completed envelope to the fuselage and handstitch (in accordance with FAA AC 43.13-1 specifications) around cutouts for fittings after attaching the envelope at tailpost and firewall. Now, using a Turkish towel or something similar, apply distilled water to tauten the fabric.

If you've used synthetic cloth (which usually goes on with the blanket, or cut-and-lap method), tautening is accomplished with an electric iron with the thermostat set on Rayon. Keep the iron moving.

When the fabric is completely dry, apply two coats of "half-and-half," half nitrate dope and half thinner. You may want to add anti-mildew powder to the first coat. In all but the driest of climates it's worth the slight extra expense. In any case, the first coat requires the most care, because it should be brushed into the fabric weave for good penetration, yet you must guard against it dripping through from the inside, especially around holes cut for fittings. Subsequent coats of clear dope (it takes six altogether for a nice finish) should be applied as thick as conditions will allow. Temperature should be at least 72 degrees F, more if humidity is high. If humidity is very high, you may not be able to dope at all. Dope will "blush"—turn a foggy white—if it does not dry uniformly through its full depth. A blushed finish has very little protective or tautening value. When the relative humidity is such that only a small amount of blushing is apparent, the condition may be eliminated by thinning the dope with a retarder. Retarder is expensive, however, and its value limited. It's usually best to simply wait for better drying conditions. Brush coats of clear dope should be cut with just enough thinner to prevent pulling or "roping." Usually, about 10% thinner works best. We do not recommend that you spray on the clear dope, because the use of a spray gun requires that you use significantly more thinner, and this results in a slower build-up and less tautening.

After the second coat of clear dope is on the envelope you must not be alarmed if the thing looks a little baggy again. As the third coat dries, it'll all tauten-up once again.

Following the third coat, sand lightly with # 180 emery paper, and be very careful when sanding over longerons, stringers, or anywhere the fabric touches the structure.

Next, put on the pinked tape and reinforcing patches as the fabric starts to tauten following the third coat. A heavy coat of dope,

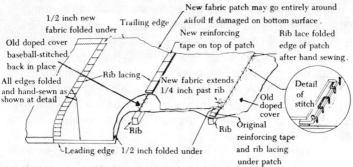

1/2 inch new fabric folded under

Trailing edge

New fabric patch may go entirely around airfoil if damaged on bottom surface.

New reinforcing tape on top of patch

Rib lace folded edge of patch after hand sewing.

Old doped cover baseball-stitched back in place

All edges folded and hand-sewn as shown at detail

Rib lacing

New fabric extends 1/4 inch past rib

Old doped cover

Detail of stitch

Rib

Rib

Original reinforcing tape and rib lacing under patch

Leading edge   1/2 inch folded under

Replacing large section of wing cover.

slightly wider than the tape, should be brushed on as far ahead as it will stay wet, while you apply the tapes over every place the fabric comes in contact with the structure underneath, or wherever the fabric *can* contact the underlying structure through vibration. Work out air bubbles with your fingers; do not pull the tape, and make sure that all the pinked edges are smoothed down.

Referencing the old fabric, make reinforcing patches for around openings for control cables and tailwheel controls from duck, twill, or Naugahyde. Dope these into place, but do *not* cut the holes for the cables. This is the last thing you do, after the final finish coats are on. Then re-dope the tapes and patches to tauten them and to fill their weave to match that of the fabric. Sand the pinked edges to feather them into the fill on the fabric.

A useful tool to have at hand during the clear dope build-up process is suggested by veteran aircraft restorers Ruth and Warren Spencer in their TAB Book No. 2203, *Aircraft Dope & Fabric*. This tool is the venerable "plumber's friend," and the Spencers use it to pull the fabric free from any underlying structural member that it is not intentionally attached to. Do not use it on wet dope, of course, but after the surface is dry to the touch. Then, as the fabric dries completely it will tighten up and remain clear of these internal parts. As the Spencers point out, to allow dope-soaked fabric to lie on wood or metal parts may result in the eventual lifting of varnish from wood, or zinc chromate from aluminum or steel; and besides, the fabric is not free to tauten evenly. To lift stuck fabric with a pin leaves holes that never close and fill, because the fabric tautens *away* from the pin-holes.

It takes a full six coats of clear dope to give a gloss, with sanding after alternate coats.

Some fabric-covered airplanes will have inspection holes in the fuselage like those on the undersides of the wings, and the plastic reinforcement rings that encircle these holes must go on the fabric after the reinforcing tapes are in place and before the fourth coat of clear dope is brushed-on. The inspection holes inside the plastic rings will not be cut out until after all dope, color included, is finished.

However, if you are installing seaplane-type drain grommets in the wings, and perhaps at the bottom of the tailpost for good drainage and internal ventilation, the small holes must be cut and the seaplane grommets cemented into place *prior* to the final coats of clear dope. Carefully dope around these grommets with the final coats, because they are soluble in dope. Seaplane grommets cost only a few cents more than the ordinary kind and are far better because their aft-facing opening creates a suction that ventilates the interior structure and helps keep it dry.

Covering Wings & Tail Surfaces

Wings and control surfaces, and usually the fin will require some form of attachment to the ribs or structure, and again the old covering will come in handy as a guide. The manner in which the fabric is attached to these members varies—rib-stitching, screws, or clips—but in any case, stick to the method used by the manufacturer. If screws are called for, as they are, for example, to attach the fabric to the wing ribs on an Aeronca Champion, you'll want to carefully measure their spacing and positioning on the old cover. If your wings require rib-stitching, reference the old cover (or a plane just like yours) and follow the FAA-approved method as detailed in the FAA publication, *Aircraft Inspection & Repair*, AC 43.13-1A&2, a necessary book that tells aircraft mechanics how everything *is to be*, though not necessarily how to do it. (See accompanying illustrations.) This book, technically an "Advisory Circular," despite its 233 pages, is available from the U.S. Government Printing Office, Washington, D.C., or from the Aviation Maintenance Foundation, which currently prices it at $7.25.

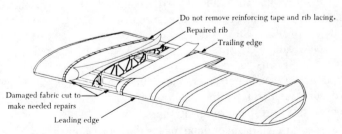

Opening cover for internal structural repair.

Before the attachments are made, a special reinforcement tape (not the same as pinked tape) is doped in place. Short pieces are used on the tail, and over each wing rib, on both top and bottom of the wing. The reinforcing tapes go on after the third coat of clear dope has begun to set-up.

Assuming that your craft requires rib-stitching, carefully measure, and mark with pencil the exact location of every stitch across each wing rib on both top and bottom surfaces. This is tedious work, but it'll speed up things later and give you professional results. You will note that the stitches within the slipstream area are twice as close together as those on outboard portions of the wing, as are the first couple of stitches at the leading edge. The stitching will be easier if you'll punch all the holes first, both top and bottom, and suspend the wing panel, leading edge down, from overhead rafters. Then recruit a helper to work on the opposite side and return the needle through the proper hole on each stitch.

With the rib-stitching completed, you are ready to install the pinked tapes. Generally speaking, put tapes over all rib-stitching, around the leading and trailing edges, chordwise. Then spanwise along the trailing edge, wingtip and butt ribs; and completely around the tail-surface edges.

With your clear dope build-up completed—the same as on the fuselage—you are ready for the silver dope. And this is when you can switch to a spray gun for best results.

Color Finishing

Whatever your final paint scheme may be, you will always follow the clear dope build-up with two coats of silver dope. Primarily, the silver undercoat is protection from the sun for the fabric. You can buy silver dope ready-mixed, or you can buy the silver powder, mix it with a little thinner to get a thin paste, and add that to uncut clear dope.

A spray gun is desirable from this point, and this means thinning the dope. Depending upon air pressure available (you need to maintain 50-60 lbs at the nozzle), temperature/humidity, and your spray equipment, your mix (in a five-gallon wide-mouth can) will contain from 40% to 60% thinner. Pour the dope through a paper strainer, and open the water-drain outlet at the pressure regulator on the air compressor *often* to prevent condensed moisture from entering the spray gun.

A spray coat of silver dope means that you cover the area in one direction, working back and forth with the nozzle about eight to ten inches above the surface; then go back over the same area at 90 degrees to the original direction. This may be regarded as two coats; but, one or two, this is the way to do it to get an even spread. And while two such applications are regarded as the minimum, you may apply up to four coats of silver for a better, glossier finish. The dope should go on wet; if it is too dry, your pressure is too high. Move the gun just fast enough to prevent runs, and don't swing the gun with your wrist because that varies the coverage.

Sand the final coat of silver with #400 emery paper; wipe clean with a soft cloth damp with thinner; then, for a deep gloss finish, here's a secret unknown to many: spray on a coat of *clear* dope cut with 20 to 25% thinner.

Finally, the color; and again we find ourselves in total agreement with the expert Spencers: "As with many tasks, the actual job is easy; it is the preparation that is slow and difficult."

It helps to make trial and error color sketches on scale three-views. Have them where they may be studied at leisure. Very often, just a slight change of angle or contour of a trim line will make a great change and improvement. Don't forget to include the bottom of the airplane; that is the part seen by everyone but you. Study color samples. Study other airplanes to determine just what it is that you do or do not like about their appearance, especially those similar to your own type. This is often a very elusive thing. Areas of darker color look more massive and heavy. Bright colors are more "agressive" and tend to dominate. A band *around* a long fuselage can interrupt the length and thereby tend to reduce the appearance of great length.

Mask the component parts one at a time (control surfaces are always removed for repainting an airplane). Masking tape should not be left for long on fresh silver dope before spraying. If there is to be only trim color over silver, mask everything except where the trim color will go.

If there is to be only limited trim over another base color, spray the base color over all. Allow it to dry, then mask everything except where the trim color will go. There is one exception: If white is used with red, do not spray red where the white is to go; reds have the unpleasant characteristic of bleeding through white. Reds can be used over white, but never white over reds. If white trim is to be used with a red base, mask and spray separately.

If there is to be a two-color combination of approximately equal areas on any component, mask one and then spray, then mask the other and spray. Allow sufficient drying time between colors before masking over the fresh dope so the masking tape will not lift it; one day between colors is enough time.

For any additional trim such as the numbers or pin-striping in a third color, *all* previously sprayed parts must be well masked.

Adhesive-backed masking stencils are available for the 12-inch numbers, and they are far superior to anything you are likely to achieve masking by hand. Decorative numbers are not legal. If your airplane happens to be 30 years old or older, it is classified as an antique by the FAA and may have small registration numerals on the rudder instead of the regulation 12-inchers on fuselage. This exception has been allowed since the late sixties, although many people seem unaware of it. All numerals must be of a contrasting color to that of fuselage or rudder. With good planning, even fuselage numbers may sometimes be used to enhance the paint scheme and overall appearance. Plan the sequence in advance so all the areas of each color used will be done at the same time with the same batch of dope.

Newspapers are all right for masking, but use double layers; wet dope will go through only one sheet. Be sure to put masking tape

One needn't be a licensed airplane mechanic to re-upholster an airplane. In fact, the shop that re-covered your living room sofa will probably do the best job.

over all the little holes along the edges of newsprint made from rolling through the presses. Mask any little tears and any gaps where dope could blow through or under. Press down all edges of the tape securely along the paint line. Do not mask very fresh, soft dope, because the tape removal may lift off the base color and even the silver. Allow at least overnight for one color to set up before masking for the next. Do not leave tape on freshly doped surfaces any longer than necessary. When removing masking tape, pull *away* from the line of freshly applied dope after giving it time to set. Watch out for drafts. Don't try to spray when the humidity is high, or when the temperature is less than 72 degrees F.

CHAPTER 4
SYNTHETIC FABRICS

There are presently available only two basic types of synthetic fabric covering materials for aircraft. One is a fiberglass cloth which is tautened (to a degree) with conventional aircraft dope, usually butyrate. The second is heat-shrinkable synthetic fabric which needs only to be coated for protection, rather than tautened with dope as is the case with cotton, Irish linen and fiberglass.

Three of the most common heat-shrinkable synthetic fabrics available are a polyamide, marketed as nylon, an acrylic fiber marketed under the trade name Orlon, and a polyester fiber marketed by Dupont under the trade name Dacron. Normally, these heat-shrinkable fabrics are cleaned and heat-shrunk by fabric finishers after weaving and before being released for distribution. However, when the raw, unfinished fabric *greige* is heat-shrunk on an airframe, a very taut covering results in a few minutes without the application of conventional aircraft dope.

Dacron has evolved as the most popular synthetic aircraft fabric to date, and when used properly will provide the best service life with the least problems of all covering materials available. Dacron can be installed on the airframe, heat-shrunk, and coated faster and with less chance of mistake, than any other covering method. Dacron griege will shrink approximately 10% and is controlled by heat application with a household iron. Sulfuric acid electrolyte from conventional lead/acid batteries, or agricultural chemicals will not deteriorate Dacron as they do cotton and linen. Dacron is not attacked by fungus in tropical climates like organic fibers and does not require fungicide additives in the coatings.

Nylon and Orlon have not proven to be a satisfactory covering material for aircraft due to a fast deterioration rate or excessive elasticity.

Contrary to some claims there is no such thing as a "lifetime" aircraft covering process. Fiberglass fabric does not deteriorate; but in actual service the dope-tautened surfaces are easily damaged because the fiberglass threads are brittle and will not stretch to absorb impact as do Dacron, cotton, and linen. The adhesion of dope to the coarse fabric styles, when applied by spray gun to avoid disturbing the weave, is minimum. The finer weave fiberglass fabric styles which can be doped with a brush for a better penetration are very difficult to tauten and often go back into service with wrinkles and ripples. Deterioration of the dope coating, poor dope adhesion, and the general appearance of the finished covering are the major causes of fiberglass cloth being removed, rather than any loss of strength of the fabric itself.

Exposure tests, conducted by Stits Aircraft (now, *there's* a respected name in aviation for more than four decades), verified that Dacron cloth will deteriorate in direct proportion to exposure to the ultraviolet rays from the sun. Bare Dacron test panels deteriorated in eight months from exposure to the sun in Southern California. Bare cotton and Irish linen panels deteriorated in three to four months. Applying this ratio, it seems reasonable to expect Dacron covering to last at least twice as long as cotton or linen covering under identical exposure conditions. Years of experience have shown that cotton and linen covering on an aircraft lasts three to 12 years, depending upon the quality of the doped finish, and the degree of protection given them from the sun.

Aircraft-Grade Dacron (Stits Poly-Fiber)

The amount of Dacron fabric used for aircraft covering is very small compared to other commercial uses of Dacron. Therefore, the fabric styles that were first adapted to cover aircraft were selected from standard styles manufactured in large quantities for other purposes. To best serve the purposes for which they were originally intended these fabrics are coarse and have an uneven thread-count, possessing more threads per inch in one direction than the other. As many aircraft mechanics have found, the problem with an uneven thread count is the uneven shrink and the uneven strength in each direction. These stock fabrics are woven with a twisted thread rather than a flat or untwisted thread which will produce a smoother surface and allow dope penetration between the fibers of each thread for better adhesion.

Stits' experience with the twisted versus untwisted thread fabric, making a 90-degree peel test with a one-inch wide Dacron finishing tape, indicated that the adhesion of the untwisted thread was one pound stronger than the twisted thread using the same cement.

Since Stits is a volume supplier of aircraft fabric, they contracted with a major mill to weave for them, exclusively, a smooth "square" fabric weave, with untwisted thread, in two weight styles (3.7 and 2.7 ounces per square yard), which shrinks proportionately in both directions, allows a better dope penetration, and fills quicker to smoother finished surface. The Stits Poly-Fiber is the only Dacron under three ounces per square yard approved by the FAA as a replacement for Grade A cotton at this time.

The Stits D-101A Dacron Poly-Fiber (3.7 oz sq yd) has an average strength of 130 lbs per inch width. It is a heavy duty cloth used for maximum life expectancy. The D-103 style (2.7 oz sq yd) has an average strength of 95 lbs per inch width, and is used when a minimum covering weight and very smooth finish are desired.

Grade A cotton weighs four ounces per square yard.

The coatings (Poly-Dope) developed by Stits for Dacron weigh approximately the same as conventional nitrate or butyrate dope film with the equal thickness. And though Poly-Dope costs more than butyrate, less Poly-Dope is used and labor is less.

In 1971, Stits sucessfully completed an extensive test program to obtain FAA approval of cemented seams in their fabric as a substitute for sewn seams on all aircraft regardless of the red line (VNe) speed. A two-inch overlap splice, covered with a two-inch finishing tape, is used on the wings, and a one-inch overlap splice, covered with a two-inch finishing tape, is used on all other parts of the airframe. In tension tests on a one-inch D-101A Dacron-to-Dacron Stits cemented (Poly-Tak) seam, the fabric always failed first.

Dacron Coatings

Dacron fabric has been in service as an aircraft covering material since the late fifties, but for a long time no really compatible coating existed to provide the flexibility, adhesion, repairability, and durability needed to match the potential service life of the Dacron itself.

Due to the lack of a more suitable or more readily available coating, conventional aircraft dope has been commonly used. The adhesion of butyrate dope to Dacron fabric is not satisfactory; therefore, three or four coats of nitrate dope, which has better adhesion, is applied first and then finished with butyrate. This combination is intended to provide the best compromise for adhesion and durability. Nitrate dope is of course highly flammable. Butyrate less so.

Now, before the polyester (Dacron) thread can be woven into a fabric it must be lubricated to process through the looms. The lubricating oil accounts for approximately 2/10 of 1% of the total weight of the Dacron fabric. (Diethylene glycol is one of the conditioning and lubricating agents used by the mills.) The raw Dacron also picks up considerable oil drippings from loom machinery. The smooth surface and presence of a lubricant are two of the reasons for the poor adhesion of nitrate and butyrate dope to Dacron griege.

Butyrate dope continues to shrink with age, and heavy finish-coats on heat-tautened Dacron will eventually distort the airframe. The use of non-tautening butyrate dope, which is made with additional proportions of plasticizers, Triphenyl phosphate, and tricresyl phosphate, helps eliminate the over-taut problem—until the plasticizers have aged in the hot sun for two or three years.

Tests on a high-solids blue-dyed nitrate dope, and a semitautening aluminum-pigmented butyrate dope labeled and sold as a Dacron-proofer, and a spray-filler, indicate only a slight improvement.

Butyrate and nitrate dope are best used for the purpose they were developed, as tautening and finish coatings on cotton and Irish linen fabric.

So, the Stits Poly-Dope coatings were developed to meet the exacting requirements of a suitable heat-shrinkable synthetic fabric coating. They cut through the oil coating on the fibers and provide over twice the adhesive strength of conventional nitrate dope and will not support a flame after all solvents have evaporated. The peel resistance of a two-inch finishing tape applied with Stits Poly-Brush is seven to nine pounds (the peel resistance of nitrate dope is one to four pounds, depending upon the application technique). And unlike conventional, fast-burning nitrocellulose fabric cements, Poly-Tak cement not only makes a bond stronger than the fabric itself, but also provides excellent adhesion to bare aluminum, glass, and a wide variety of materials.

The flexibility of the non-tautening Poly-Dope coatings allows the loads to be carried by the heat-tautened fabric, rather than by the finish. A finish under tension is more subject to cracking with age than an inert, stable finish.

Stits Poly-Tone is the standard pigmented finish for this covering process. Poly-Tone is non-tautening, non-bleeding, fire-retardent, chemical resistant, used on both metal and fabric, is easily refinished or repaired, air dries to a satin gloss, and may be polished to a high luster. Stits also offers Aero-Thane, a two-part, tough, flexible urethane enamel formulated especially for a high-gloss finish on fabric surfaces, fabric-covered wood surfaces, laminated fiberglass, and metal components of fabric-covered aircraft.

Automotive & Industrial Finishes on Aircraft Fabric

There have been many types of automotive and industrial finishes used on aircraft fabric, usually because they were the only type finishes with a wide range of colors available in the area at the time; none have been completely satisfactory. Epoxy paint, nitrocellulose lacquer, and acrylic lacquer are too brittle for successful use on fabric surface and will crack after a short time, depending upon the fabric flexing in service and exposure conditions. The finish on an aircraft tied-down outside in the Southwest will deteriorate considerably faster than in the northeastern states or when stored in a hangar.

Synthetic enamel is the most common automotive finish used on aircraft fabric. It is more weather resistant than pigmented nitrate or butyrate dope finish, and dries to a good gloss; but it will become brittle in a shorter length of time in sunlight due to oxidation of the vegetable oils it contains.

Synthetic enamel was developed in the thirties to replace lacquer as an automotive metal finish, and was not intended to be used on flexible fabric surfaces. It is an alkyd resin and is not compatible with the solvents used in nitrate and butyrate dope, lacquer, or the Stits Poly-Dopes. When synthetic enamel is overcoated with any of these materials, the solvents penetrate and swell or "lift" the enamel. To make suitable fabric repairs, the synthetic enamel coat is removed.

There are many manufacturers of synthetic (alkyd) enamel, each with his own particular formula depending upon the proposed end use. However, the basic characteristics of synthetic enamel are the same whether labeled automotive, industrial, or aircraft enamel.

An often used quickie method of two or three coats of nitrate dope on Dacron, three coats of aluminum pigmented butyrate dope, then five or six heavy coats of automotive metal primer, each sanded to completely hide the fabric weave and tapes, then a finish of automotive synthetic enamel will look beautiful—for about a year.

Then the primer and enamel starts to peel from the aluminum pigmented butyrate dope. Unequal thermal expansion and incompatible solvent systems coupled with oxidation and decreasing flexibility of the enamel, are the causes.

Cross linking (two-part) polyurethane enamels which have been formulated for the most durable finish on metal surfaces are by necessity very hard, and by characteristics very smooth and glossy, and will look very good on fabric surfaces. However, these will eventually crack because they will not take the continued flexing imposed on fabric surfaces. Urethane enamel finishes cannot be rejuvenated, and complete stripping is the only practical procedure to eliminate any cracking problem.

CHAPTER 5

PAINTING METAL AIRCRAFT

Aluminum and magnesium alloys in particular are protected originally by a variety of surface treatments. Steels may have been
"Parco Lubrized" or otherwise oxidized on the surface during man-
ufacture. Most of these coatings can only be restored by processes
which are completely impractical in the field. But corroded areas
where such protective films have been destroyed require some type
of treatment prior to refinishing. The following inhibiting materials
are particularly effective in the field treatment of aluminum, are
beneficial to bare magnesium, and are of some value even on bare
steel parts.

The labels on the containers of surface treatment chemicals will
offer warnings if a material is toxic or flammable. However, the label
may not be large enough to accommodate a list of all the hazards
which may ensue if the material is mixed with incompatible substances. For example, some chemicals used in surface treatments
will react violently if inadvertently mixed with paint thinners. Chemical surface treatment materials must be handled with extreme care
and mixed exactly according to directions.

Chromic Acid Inhibitor

A ten percent solution by weight of chromic acid, activated by a
small amount of sulfuric acid, is particularly effective in treating
exposed or corroded aluminum surfaces. It may also be used to treat
corroded magnesium.

This treatment tends to restore the protective oxide coating on the metal surface. Such treatment must be followed by regular paint finishes as soon as practicable, and never later than the same day as the latest chromic acid treatment. Chromium trioxide flake is a powerful oxidizing agent and a fairly strong acid. It must be stored away from organic solvents and other combustibles. Wiping cloths used in chromic-acid pickup should either be rinsed thoroughly after use or disposed of.

Sodium Dichromate Solution

A less active chemical mixture for surface treatment of aluminum is a solution of sodium dichromate and chromic acid. Entrapped solutions of this mixture are less likely to corrode metal surfaces than chromic acid inhibitor solutions.

Chemical Surface Treatments

Several commercial, activated chromic acid mixtures are available under Specification MIL-C-5541 for field treatment of damaged or corroded aluminum surfaces. Precautions should be taken to make sure that sponges or cloths used are thoroughly rinsed to avoid a possible fire hazard after drying.

Dry-Cleaning Solvent

Stoddard solvent is the most common petroleum-base solvent used in aircraft cleaning. Its flashpoint is slightly above the 105 degrees F recommended minimum, and it may be used to remove grease, oils, or light soils. Dry-cleaning solvent is preferable to kerosene for all cleaning purposes, but like kerosene it leaves a slight residue upon evaporation which may interfere with the application of some final paint films.

Aliphatic and Aromatic Naphtha

Aliphatic naphtha is recommended for wipe-down of cleaned surfaces just before painting. This material can also be used for cleaning acrylics and rubber; but it flashes at approximately 80 degrees F and must be used with care.

Aromatic naphtha should not be confused with the aliphatic material. Aromatic naphtha is toxic and attacks acrylics and rubber products, and must be used with adequate controls.

Safety Solvent

Safety solvent, trichloroethane (methyl chloroform), is used for general cleaning and grease removal. It is nonflammable under ordinary circumstances, and is used as a replacement for carbon tetrachloride. The use and safety precautions necessary when using chlorinated solvents must be observed. Prolonged use can cause dermatitis on some people.

Methyl Ethyl Ketone (MEK)

MEK is also available as a solvent cleaner for metal surfaces and paint stripper for small areas. This is a very active solvent and metal cleaner, with a flashpoint of about 24 degrees F. It is toxic when inhaled, and safety precautions must be observed during its use.

Aluminum Surface Painting Procedure

In most cases, the decision on the painting preparation sequence is a compromise between the allowable painting budget and paint service requirements. However, a little more attention to details of the metal surface preparation can be the difference between paint problems developing in six months, or the paint remaining in excellent condition for six to ten years or longer.

The so called *chromated* enamels used for economy reasons on aluminum without a conversion coating treatment or a primer will usually start peeling within a year. The use of non-corrosion inhibiting primers on top of an inadequately cleaned and treated surface is also a common cause of paint film loss or corrosion developing under the paint film in humid climates, indicated by blisters. Workmanship is 95% of a good paint job.

Thorough cleaning by Scotch-Brite scrubbing and a chromic acid conversion treatment is the recommended minimum preparation for a reasonable service life from *any* paint system on aluminum surfaces which will be exposed to the elements. Phosphoric acid etch before chromic acid treatment is recommended when severe environmental conditions are expected.

Now, since the two-part polyurethane enamels, such as the Stits Aluma-Thane (applied over a properly prepared surface), are probably the most durable of all finishes for metal aircraft, we will detail their application.

Old Painted Surfaces

Mask any area which will be damaged by paint stripper using cloth masking tape and polyethylene plastic sheet or equivalent material. Strip the old finish and thoroughly clean with Scotch-Brite abrasive pads or fine aluminum wool using water as a lubricant. Never use steel wool or emery cloth on aluminum surfaces. Any aluminum surface corrosion, indicated by discoloring and scaling, should be treated with Stits Aluma-Dyne E-2310 or E-2311 phosphoric acid etch and brightner while scrubbing to show new metal. Phosphoric acid treatment of the entire surface after scrubbing is recommended and serves to provide microscopic tooth adhesion and a very clean surface for the primer bond. After etching, thoroughly rinse all acid from the surfaces with clean running water or clean rags rung-out in clean water. Do not rinse with hot water. Air-blow hinges, seams, and joints which may trap acid.

Bare Oxidized Surfaces

Surfaces heavily coated with oil, dirt, or mud should be cleaned with Stits XOFF-310 alkaline cleaner. After alkaline cleaning, mask any adjacent areas or openings which may be damaged by acid contact. Old oxidized aluminum surfaces should be scrubbed with Scotch-Brite abrasive pads using diluted XOFF-310 alkaline cleaner as a lubricant, then treated with Aluma-Dyne E-2310 or E-2311 phosphoric acid etch. Pitted or corroded areas should be scrubbed while etching to show new metal. Thoroughly rinse and dry as described above.

New Aluminum Surfaces

Remove all dirt, light oxidation, oil, and residue of any protective coating by scrubbing with Scotch-Brite pads using diluted XOFF-310 as a lubricant. Wash with clean water (cold), dry, mask as needed, and treat with phosphoric acid etch as explained above.

Treat all aluminum surfaces with Stits Aluma-Dyne E-2300 chromic acid conversion coating before the surface becomes contaminated or within eight hours after etching or Scotch-Brite scrubbing. Use a nylon brush or cellulose sponge and *wear rubber gloves along with a face shield*. If more than eight hours elapses before chromic acid treatment, repeat the phosphoric acid etch or scrubbing operation. After the chromic acid treatment, wash with clean, cold water and dry with clean rags. Air-blow all water from hinges, joints and seams or allow to evaporate. Chromic acid is not harmful if trapped in joints or seams.

Wipe all surfaces with a clean, untreated, lint-free, knit-type wiping or polishing cloth, or similar paper wipe towels, wetted with Stits C-2200 Metl-Sol cleaner just before priming. Shop towels furnished by commercial towel services are not recommended for final cleaning because they often contain silicones from previous polishing operations which are released by strong solvents and spread over the metal surface.

The original paint scheme on this 1964 Cessna 150 is unimaginative by today's standards. Plan your colors with three-view scale drawings and take your time deciding.

Apply two coats of Stits EP-420 corrosion-resistant epoxy primer before the chromic acid treated surfaces become contaminated and preferably within 24 hours after chromic acid treatment. Recommended primer dry film thickness is 0.6 to 1.0 mils. If the epoxy primer has aged more than three days before recoating, it should be scuff-sanded with Scotch-Brite pads or 400-grit Wetordry (3M) sandpaper to remove the glaze and provide tooth adhesion. Avoid heavy scratches which will show through the high gloss finish coat.

The use of a pre-treatment Wash Primer (vinyl butyral-phosphoric acid resin) before application of the intermediate primer is recommended for the best protection and will improve paint service life in very humid or rainy climates or on components subject to water submersion. Wash Primer must be applied within the seven-hour elapsed time specified after mixing, and recoated with the intermediate primer within 24 hours after application. Vinyl butyral wash primers are not considered to have sufficient pigment loading or film thickness to be used as a sole primer coat. An intermediate coat of conventional primer, such as Epoxy EP-420 primer, is recommended before the finished coat.

Apply the selected finish coat before the primed surfaces have become contaminated. Any inadvertent contamination, such as fingerprints or oil, may be safely removed with Stits C-2210 Paint Surface Cleaner. Remove any dust or lint from the primer surface with a clean, good quality tack rag just before painting. We recommend three coats of Stits Aluma-Thane enamel at 15 to 20 minute intervals, allowing sufficient time between coats to avoid runs.

Many professional painters prefer to apply the lighter colors, such as yellows, light blues, light reds, etc., over a white base coat to enhance the color shade. The white base coat should dry thoroughly before applying the color coat to eliminate the possibility of the fresh white pigments migrating to the surface of the color coat. (We should note that the Stits urethane enamels do not have the crawling and cratering characteristics inherent in some other brands of urethane enamels in the market.)

Recommended finish coat thickness is 1.3 to 2.0 mils, depending upon the type of coating. The higher solids epoxy primer and urethane finishes will build a thicker film with each coat than the one part coatings and primers.

Steel Surface Painting Procedure

The steel surface must be free of all rust oil, grease, tar, wax, and old paint scale to provide good adhesion and prevent corrosion development under the primer. Excessively dirty and grimy surfaces should be thoroughly cleaned. Stits Metl-Sol C-2200 Cleaner will remove light oil, grease, wax, silicone, and tar. Heavy rust, corrosion, and paint scale should be removed with sand or glass-bead blasting.

Working small areas, treat the cleaned surface with Aluma-Dyne E-2310 phosphoric acid etch solution, diluted with equal parts of water or full strength, depending upon the surface condition. Use a nylon brush or cellulose sponge and wear rubber gloves and a face shield. Scrub with steel wool pads or a wire brush during the acid etch treatment to remove any light rust and scale. The acid solution should remain on the steel surface for five minutes, and then the surface is washed thoroughly with clean running water or wiped with clean rags wrung-out in clean water. Wipe dry with clean rags and air-blow all corners, joints, and seams to remove any acid etch residue.

Within a few hours after the etched steel surface is dried, apply two coats of EP-420 Corrosion Resistant Epoxy Primer. Do not allow the surface to become contaminated before primer application. (The use of a pre-treatment wash primer—vinyl butyral-phosphoric acid resin—before application of the intermediate primer is optional and will improve the paint service life in humid weather and on components subject to water submersion.)

After the primer has dried, apply the finish coats.

Treating Oxidized or Corroded Aluminum Not to be Painted

Surfaces heavily coated with oil, dirt, or mud should be cleaned with XOFF-310 alkaline cleaner. Then mask any adjacent areas or openings which may be damaged by acid contact, using cloth masking tape and polyethylene plastic sheeting.

Working a limited area to provide adequate attention and time control, apply Aluma-Dyne E-2311 phosphoric acid cream or E-2310 phosphoric acid solution with a nylon brush or cellulose sponge. Wear rubber gloves and a face shield. Excessively oxidized, stained, or corroded surfaces should be scrubbed with Scotch-Brite Ultra-fine cleaning pads while etching to show new metal. Never use steel wool or emery cloth on aluminum surfaces because they leave microscopic particles that promote corrosion.

Thoroughly rinse with cool running water or wipe with wet rags or sponge wrung-out in clean water. Then air-blow hinges, seams, and joints where acid may be trapped.

Allow the surface to dry, or wipe dry with clean rags, and proceed with the chromic acid treatment before the surface becomes contaminated or within a maximum of eight hours after the phosphoric acid etch or scrubbing. The Aluma-Dyne E-2300 chromic acid treatment is recommended for corrosion protection whether the surface is to remain bare, be waxed, or painted with a clear finish.

When a bright polished finish is desired, the surface should be buffed *before* the invisible Aluma-Dyne treatment. Remove any buffing compound residue with XOFF-310 cleaner before the chromic acid treatment. Add one spoon of XOFF-310 to 16 ounces of diluted chromic acid solution to break the water surface tension and provide improved flow out on the polished aluminum surface. Use this modified chromic acid within seven days or throw it out. Do not polish the surface with an abrasive after the chromic acid treatment or the invisible protective coating will be removed.

Corrosion Protection for Interior & Inaccessible Areas

Interior surfaces which need corrosion protection from salt water, such as floats, wings, or aft fuselage, may be alkaline cleaned, chromic acid treated, and small cloth bags of potassium dichromate or sodium dichromate placed in strategic locations where water may pool. Secure the bags to avoid interference with any controls, and replace as needed.

The diluted XOFF-310 Alkaline Cleaner is sprayed through inspection access holes and any other openings with an engine wash gun. Follow with a clean water rinse and allow to drain.

Dilute the chromic acid solution at a ratio of one part to three parts clean water and spray the interior with an engine wash gun in the same manner. Wear rubber gloves and face mask. If the component can be removed to handle, flush by rotating. A plastic sheet over supporting structures forming a trough will contain the spilled and reusable solution. Complete rinsing of the interior after 10 to 15 minutes is optional because the chromic acid solution is harmless after it is spent. After the chromic acid solution is thoroughly drained, drying may be aided by an air blast through the interior.

Painting Interior Surfaces

Interior aluminum surfaces, in good condition, which are to be painted only for cosmetic purposes, may be cleaned with C-2200 Metl-Sol Cleaner or XOFF-310 Alkaline Cleaner and primed. Interior surfaces which will be exposed to corrosive elements such as sea water, should be cleaned, scrubbed, and treated with Aluma-Dyne chromic acid conversion coating before priming.

Finishing Fiberglass Components

Strip any old paint or primer film; thoroughly clean, and sand with 320 grit Wetordry (3M) sandpaper. New surfaces should be cleaned of any mold release coatings using an appropriate solvent, depending upon the type of mold release used. Silicone types may be removed with C-2200 Metl-Sol Cleaner. Sand thoroughly with 320 Wetordry to remove the surface gloss and provide tooth adhesion.

Apply one good coat of Stits EP-420 epoxy primer, and finish with three coats of Aluma-Thane enamel. If the epoxy primer has aged more than three days before recoating, scuff-sand to remove the primer surface gloss.

Paint Quality

There are many brands of zinc chromate primers on the market, and it should be noted that zinc chromate is only a corrosion inhibiting dry pigment which must be incorporated in a suitable "vehicle" or resin to provide adhesion and bond the zinc chromate pigments to the metal surfaces. One of the most common vehicles used is based on low-cost oil alkyd resins. The better quality alkyd primers manufactured to MIL-P-8585 specifications provide good service on most commercial applications. However, many economy brands of alkyd primers are not compatible with the solvents in the polyurethane enamels and may "lift."

And while our own experience dictates that we recommend the two part polyurethane enamels as the most durable finishes for metal aircraft, we should mention that exposure to light urethane enamel spray mist for as little as 30 minutes will give many people the symptoms of flu the following day. Persons with respiratory ailments have been hospitalized after breathing urethane spray mist, and it should be assumed that heavy exposure could be fatal. Therefore, a plastic eye shield and face filter mask (activated charcoal or hood with fresh air supply) should be worn when spray painting with the polyurethane enamels.

Epoxy primers are considered superior to all other types of primers, and provide better adhesion to aluminum surfaces than do urethane primers. Urethane primers do give slightly more chemical and solvent resistance than epoxy primers, but since the primer is coated with a finish it is not exposed to chemicals and solvents.

Good quality urethane finishes provide about twice the service life of epoxy finishes. Epoxy finishes are usually about as durable as synthetic enamel and will "chalk" in about the same length of time. However, epoxy finishes give far better chemical and solvent resistance than synthetic enamel. Tests by major suppliers, here and abroad, reveal that the best paint system for metal aircraft is epoxy primers and urethane finish coats.

Spraying Equipment & Suggestions

A DeVilbiss Model MBC-510 or JGA-501 spray gun, with a #30 air cap and EX tip and needle, may be regarded as more or less standard for aircraft coatings. Any alternate brand with equivalent air cap and needle size, either pressure pot or suction type, will also provide good results. Correct adjustment of air-to-liquid is important. Be certain that the spray gun air requirement does not exceed your air supply or hose capacity.

Pressure pot painting equipment may apply up to twice the amount of material as the suction type gun on each coat. This should be taken into consideration when counting the number of coats

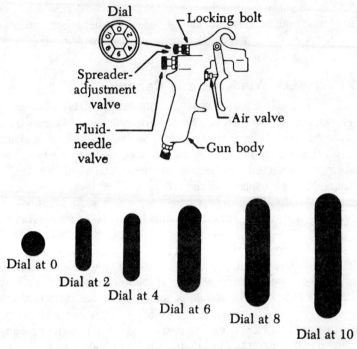

Spray patterns at various dial settings.

applied to a surface. Ten pounds of air at the pressure pot with 50 pounds of air at the gun will apply about the same amount in two coats as the suction gun will in three.

Do not intermix or substitute reducers or thinners. Filter all coatings before application.

Do not use paper cups coated with wax, or any other contaminated container to transfer, measure, or store coatings.

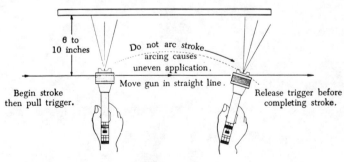

Spray gun stroke.

Do not spray paint in the following conditions: drafty, windy or dusty area; outdoors in direct sunlight if the weather is hot; outdoors in a heavy fog or when dew is forming; high humidity; below 60 degrees F or above 100 degrees F.

Windshields, Windows, and Canopies

Compounds for paint stripping, degreasing, and brightening, as well as most organic solvents, cause serious damage to transparent acrylic plastics. All such parts should be removed before starting paint stripping, and should not be replaced until the cleaning and painting is completed and the paint or lacquer thoroughly dry, since paint and lacquer cause crazing of plastics. The plastic parts should be removed from the *area* where the stripping, degreasing, or painting is being done. The parts should be protected with soft cloth covers.

If it is impractical to remove a plastic panel, cut a polyethylene sheet—minimum thickness of .010-inch and containing no pinholes—to match as exactly as possible the size of the window. The polyethylene sheet should fit snugly over the surface of the window, and the edges should be carefully taped with cloth masking tape at least two inches wide to permit at least one inch of sealing width on both the plastic film and the airframe. Make certain that no liquid or fumes can seep through to the window. It is important that the entire surface of the window be covered, and that no cutting tools be used to remove the masking.

Aluminum foil is unsatisfactory as a protection from paint and other sprays that contain solvents because of its low resistance to tears, punctures, and pinholes.

CHAPTER 6
TRANSPARENT PLASTICS

Acrylic plastics are about all that is used anymore for lightplane windows. These come in sheets of standard thickness, the most commonly used being .090, .120, .187, and .250 sizes. There are two types: the thermoplastic and thermosetting plastic. Thermoplastics are originally hard but become soft and pliable when exposed to heat. When pliable they can be molded; and, as they cool, will retain the molded shape. When heated again and allowed to cool without being restrained, thermoplastics will return to their original shape. This process may be repeated many times without damage to the material unless the specified heat ranges are exceeded.

Thermosetting plastics are molded and allowed to cool in the desired shape. No amount of reheating will cause them to become pliable and workable. Once formed, they retain that shape and cannot be re-molded.

Each of these types of transparent plastics is available in monolithic or laminated forms. Monolithic plastic sheets are made in single solid uniform sheets. Laminated plastic sheets are made from transparent plastic face sheets bonded by an inner layer of material, usually polyvinyl butyral.

In addition to their ease of fabrication and maintenance, plastics have other characteristics which make them better than glass for use in transparent enclosures. Plastics break in large, dull-edged pieces; they have low water absorption, and they do not readily fatigue-crack from vibration. On the other hand, although they are non-

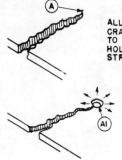

ALL THE STRAINS WHICH ORIGINALLY CAUSED CRACK ARE CONCENTRATED AT POINT Ⓐ - TENDING TO EXTEND CRACK. THEREFORE DRILL A SMALL HOLE AT END OF CRACK POINT Ⓐ1 TO DISTRIBUTE STRAIN OVER WIDER AREA.

EACH CRACK OCCURRING AT ANY HOLE OR TEAR IS DRILLED IN SAME MANNER.

Stop-drilling cracks to limit damage.

conductors of electricity, they become highly electrostatic when polished.

Plastics do not possess the surface hardness of glass, so they are more easily scratched. Since scratches will impair vision, they must be cleaned with care when servicing an airplane.

The replacement of aircraft windows is sometimes necessitated by severe crazing, apparently caused by exposure to harmful solvents and improper maintenance handling. The crazing appears as a network of cracks running in all directions over the surface of the plastic. It can also occur within the plastic at or near cemented joints.

The use of improper cleaning fluids or compounds is the most common cause of this problem. The crazing action of a solvent is often delayed; that is, crazing may not appear for several weeks after exposure to solvent or fumes.

Routine removal of film and other operational soils, where abrasive polishing for scratch removal is not required, should be done as follows:

1. Always remove rings from your fingers, then flush the plastic surface with plenty of water, using your bare hands to feel for and gently dislodge any dirt, sand, or mud.

2. Wash with mild soap and water. Be sure the water is free of harmful abrasives. A soft cloth, sponge, or chamois may be used in washing, but only to carry the soapy water to the plastic. Go over the surface with bare hands to quickly detect and remove any remaining dirt before it scratches the plastic.

3. Dry with a damp, clean chamois, a clean, soft cloth, or soft tissue. Do not continue rubbing the plastic after it is dry. This not only scratches, but will build-up an electrostatic charge that attracts dust particles. If the surface becomes

charged, patting or gently blotting with a clean, damp chamois will remove the charge and the dust.

4. Never use a coarse or rough cloth for polishing. Cheese-cloth is not acceptable.

In very hot weather, canopies, windshields, and cabin windows of parked aircraft can absorb enough heat to soften and distort them unless certain precautions are taken. If the surrounding air temperature is between 100 and 120 degrees F, enclosures should be opened enough to permit free air circulation inside the aircraft. In temperatures above 120 degrees F, the enclosures should be opened for interior circulation and protected from the sun by a suitable cover that does not come in contact with the plastic. If at all possible, the plane should be parked in the shade.

Installation Procedures

When installing a replacement panel, follow the same mounting method used by the aircraft manufacturer. Where difficulty is encountered in rivet installation, bolts may be substituted, provided that the manufacturer's original strength requirements are met and the bolts do not interfere with adjoining equipment.

In some cases replacements may not fit the installation exactly, but never force a transparent panel out of shape to make it fit a frame. If the replacement does not fit easily into the mounting, get another one, or sand the edges to obtain a proper fit. Don't heat and re-form areas of a panel, because field heating methods aren't likely to be thorough enough to reduce stress concentrations.

Fitting and handling should be done with masking material in place (that is, the protective covering on the plastic sheet). Don't scribe plastic through the masking material. On edges where the

| | Dimensional Allowance in Inches * | |
Dimension of Panel in Inches **	Required for Expansion from 25°C (77°F) to 70°C (158°F)	Required for Contraction from 25°C (77°F) to −55°C (−67°F)
12	0.031	0.050
24	0.062	0.100
36	0.093	0.150
48	0.124	0.200
60	0.155	0.250
72	0.186	0.300

*Where the configuration of a curved part is such as to take up dimensional changes by change of contour, the allowances given may be reduced if it will not result in localized stress. Installations permitting linear change at both ends require half the listed clearanced.
**For dimensions other than those given use proportional clearance.

Expansion and contraction allowances.

panels will be covered, or attached to, remove the masking material.

Since plastics expand and contract approximately three times as much as metal, suitable allowance for dimensional changes with temperature must be made. Use the values shown on the accompanying chart as minimum clearances between the frames and the plastics.

Bolt and Rivet Mountings

In bolt installations, spacers, collars, shoulders, or stop nuts should be used to prevent excessive tightening of the bolt. Whenever such devices are used by the aircraft manufacturer, they should be retained in the replacement installation.

Here are the general rules to follow:

1. Use as many bolts or rivets as practical.
2. Distribute the total stresses as equally as possible along the bolts and rivets.

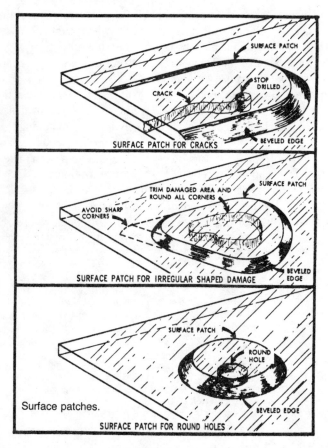

Surface patches.

3. Make sure the holes drilled in the plastic are sufficiently larger than the diameter of the bolt to permit expansion and contraction of the plastic relative to the frame.
4. Make sure the holes in the plastic are concentric with the holes in the frame so that the greater relative expansion of the plastic will not cause binding at one edge of the hole. The hole should be smooth and free of any nicks or roughness.
5. Use oversize tube spacers, shoulder bolts, rivets, cap nuts, or some other device to protect the plastic from direct pressure.

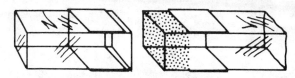

Before contact

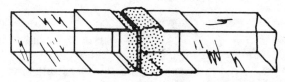

Contact only

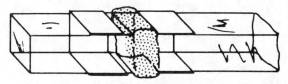

Joint under pressure

Joint "drying." Cushions harden.

Cementing with solvent cement.

Synthetic Fiber Edge Attachment

Modern edge attachments to transparent plastic assemblies are made of synthetic fibers impregnated with plastic resins. The most commonly used fibers are glass, Orlon, nylon, and Dacron.

Reinforced laminated edges attachments are the best type, especially if bolt or rivet mounted. These edges have the advantage of more efficiently distributing the load and reducing failures caused by differential thermal expansion.

Laminated edge attachments may be mounted by any of the foregoing methods, with any needed holes drilled through the edge attachment material and not the transparent plastic.

The most efficient method of mounting a laminated edge attachment is by the *slotted hole* method. The slotted holes are in the edge attachment and allow for the necessary thermal expansion.

Cellulose Acetate Base Plastics

Older aircraft may have transparent plastic enclosures made of cellulose acetate base plastic, and in general, maintenance of these is similar to that practiced with acrylic plastics. There are additional considerations.

Since the chemical composition of acetate base plastics differs greatly from that of acrylics, the cement used is of a different type. As a rule, two types are used, solvent and dope.

Solvent type cement is usually used where transparency must be maintained at the joint. It is relatively quick-drying and is well adapted for use in making emergency repairs. However, even though this cement is quick-drying, the drying time will vary with atmospheric conditions and the size of the joint. Acetone may be used as a solvent type cement.

Dope cement is preferred for use where the pieces to be joined do not conform exactly. This cement softens the surfaces of a joint and, at the same time, creates a layer between the two pieces being cemented. It does not give a transparent joint, and requires 12 to 24 hours to reach full strength.

These plastics are affected by moisture and will swell as they absorb water. In general, allow 1/8 inch per foot of panel length for expansion, and 3/16 inch per foot for contraction.

Fabricating Transparent Plastics

Although the homebuilt-airplane people often fabricate their own windshields and, by heating acrylic plastic sheets in the ovens of kitchen ranges at 275 degrees F (five minutes for each 1/16 inch thickness of the plastic), come up with all kinds of molded enclosures for their machines, you will not attempt to make your own replacement windshield for your "store-bought" airplane. Even if you possessed a proper mold and were willing to try it, it wouldn't be legal. If you need a new windshield, consign that job to your local A&P.

So, stick to side windows and other flat or nearly flat panels. These plastics may be cold-bent (single curvature) if the material is thin and the radius of curvature is at least 180 times the thickness of the sheet. For example, an 18-inch length of transparent plastic, .250 inch thick, should not be deflected more than 3/4 inch. Cold bending beyond these limits imposes stresses that will, sooner or later, usually result in crazing.

Cutting and drilling of plastics may be done with tools normally used for wood or soft metal. Where extreme accuracy is not required, the work can be laid out by pencilling the cutting lines directly on the protective masking paper. For close tolerances, however, it is advisable to inscribe layout lines directly on the surface of the plastic. Use straightedges or layout templates. If the masking paper is removed before scribing, it should be replaced to within about 1/4 inch of the scribed markings before the piece is cut.

Scribing and edge-sanding is the cutting method most generally used on flat sections or two-dimensional curved pieces. The sheet is

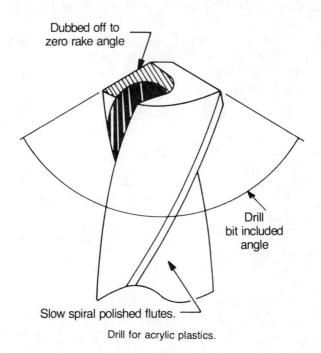

Drill for acrylic plastics.

first cut to approximate shape on a band saw, using a scribed line as a guide and cutting about 1/16 inch oversize. It's best to use disc sanders when removing material from straightedges and outside curves. Drum or belt sanders work best for inside curves. When sanding irregular shapes or larger pieces which are awkward to maneuver around a fixed machine, use a small electric hand sander.

For the sake of both accuracy and safety, hold work between a piece of plywood or hardboard on each side. The twist drills commonly used for soft metals may be used successfully.

Cementing of transparent acrylic plastics depends upon the intermingling of the two surfaces of the joint so that actual cohesion exists. This is usually accomplished by dipping one of the two pieces into the acrylic cement solvent (available from most aircraft supply houses) until a sufficient "cushion" is formed. Then, when this surface is pressed against the opposite dry surface, the excess cement forms a second cushion which permits thorough intermingling of the two surfaces.

Cracks may be repaired in acrylics by stop-drilling the ends and cementing a patch over the crack area, using a beveled edge all around. With a little more care, a flush-patch may be inserted and cemented in place. Only relatively small areas should be patched, and no repairs should be made that will in any way interfere with the pilot's vision.

Minor surface scratches are often polished out with a very fine abrasive such as jeweler's rouge or an automotive rubbing compound. And, finally, a protective coat of wax is recommended to reduce the likelihood of such scratches.

CHAPTER 7
WOODEN STRUCTURES

The aircraft with wood-framed wings and/or plywood skin should be kept in a dry, well-ventilated hangar with all inspection covers and access panels removed, for as long as possible prior to inspection. If the airplane is thoroughly dried out, this will facilitate the inspection, especially when determining the condition of gluded joints.

Before starting a careful inspection of the internal structure, a rough idea of the general condition of the structure can sometimes be gained by looking over the outside. Look for evidence of warping or any distortion that departs from the original shape.

Where light structures using single plywood covering are concerned, some slight sectional undulation or building between panels may be permissible provided the wood and glue are sound. Where such a condition exists, however, a careful check must be made of the attachment of the ply to its supporting structure.

The contours and alignment of leading and trailing edges are of particular importance. Any external distortion of these light plywood and spruce members is a sign of internal deterioration, and a careful internal inspection will have to be made for security of these parts to the main wing structure as well as for damage to these parts themselves.

Splits in the fabric covering on plywood surfaces often tip off splits in the plywood beneath, so don't just repair the fabric without first examining the underlying wood.

Your external inspection is merely a starting point, and no matter how good a wood-framed airplane may look from the outside, wood and glue deterioration may still be present inside. If moisture can get into the interior, it will seek the lowest point and, if it can't get out, will stagnate and promote rapid damage. A prime place is the wing trailing edge on taildragger airplanes. Sure, there should be drain grommets beneath the trailing edge, perhaps even the very effective seaplane-type grommets; but have they been properly placed to drain and ventilate *every* moisture-collection point? These grommets should be placed just ahead of any part that can trap moisture, including the aft part of any "boxed" section. They are advisable on both inboard and outboard sides of trailing-edge tips of all wood ribs, especially on fairly large wings. They are essential on the outboard side of all ribs in every component—outboard, because dihedral will cause moisture to drain inboard. On fabric-covered airplanes, a drain grommet is a good idea at the bottom of the tailpost.

We should also point out that glue deterioration may result from other causes without the presence of water, and the proper inspection of glued joints usually isn't easy. Even when access to the joint exists, it is still hard to positively judge the soundness of the joint.

There are enough Fairchild 24s (above), Beech Staggerwings, and others still flying to suggest that properly maintained wooden structures may be as durable as metal.

Some of the common causes of glue deterioration are: 1) Chemical reactions of the glue due to aging, moisture, extreme temperatures, or a combination of these things; 2) wood shrinkage due to age and/or temperature extremes; and 3) development of fungus growths.

Airplanes exposed to large cyclic changes of temperature and humidity are especially prone to wood shrinkage. The amount of movement of wooden members due to these changes varies with the size of each member, the rate of growth of the tree from which the wood came, and the way in which the wood was converted. Therefore, two major members in an aircraft structure, joined by glue, are unlikely to have identical characteristics. Differential loads will as a result be transmitted across the glue film since the two members will not react exactly together. This will impose stresses in the glued joint which normally is strong enough to handle such loads when the airplane is new and for some years afterwards. But remember, glue tends to deteriorate with age, and at some point, probably after ten years or more, the stresses at the glued joints may cause failure of the joints.

In fairness, we must mention that the Bellanca 260Cs and Vikings, which have been produced since the mid-sixties or thereabouts, may be expected to substantially outlast woodwinged airplanes fabricated by earlier methods. The wings of these craft are resin-dipped, then covered with mahogany plywood and finished with Dacron. Bellanca claims that their hand-built wings are both stronger and lighter than similar metal-framed wings. As far as we know, there has never been a significant AD note on them, and Bellanca says no structural failures. Ten years from now, we can make a better judgment of the Bellanca process.

However, on one occasion, several years ago, we witnessed an unscheduled test of the Viking wing's structural integrity. We were cruising at 13,000 over central Pennsylvania in a Viking 300. We were holding a heading of 165 degrees with the setting sun on our right wingtip, and had just figured our true airspeed at 206 mph. Then, suddenly, another airplane materialized out of the sun on a 90-degree collision course to us. He seemed halfway up our wing in the fraction of a second we possessed as reaction time. There was no time to think; just yank the wheel back violently in panic. It was over within the space of a couple of heartbeats—if indeed, any hearts were beating. The idiot in the Twin Comanche never saw us. We watched in dismay as he sailed merrily off into the evening haze reading his comic book or whatever else he was doing besides flying

Spruce spars and metal ribs, wire-braced, combined for strength, light weight, and flexibility in the wings of the Great Lakes 2T-1A biplane. The Lakes was long a favorite among aerobatic pilots. A modern version is now produced in Wichita.

his airplane. And we looked out at the Viking's wooden wings and silently blessed the guys that had stuck them together. We started to take out the owner's handbook and look up the Viking's maximum maneuvering speed again. Seemed to us that it was listed somewhere around 160 mph. But we put it back unopened. It really didn't make any difference.

But back to wood and glue, and the checking thereof. When checking a glue line (the edge of the glued joint) for condition, all protective varnish should be removed by careful scraping. Be very careful not to damage the wood. Stop scraping at once when down to bare wood and the glue line is clearly discernible. Use a magnifying glass to examine the glue line. Where the glue line tends to part or where the presence of glue cannot be detected or is suspect, the glue line should be probed with a thin feeler gauge. If any penetration is possible, the joint should be regarded as defective. It's important that the surrounding wood be dry; otherwise a false impression of the glue line is likely due to closing of the joint by swelling. In cases where pressure is exerted on a joint, either by the surrounding structure or by metal attachment devices such as bolts or screws, you can also get a false impression of the glue condition unless the joint is relieved of this pressure.

Wood Condition

There are a lot of "Gray Eagle" types around who will tell you that Aircraft Grade spruce—especially, Sitka spruce—is unequalled

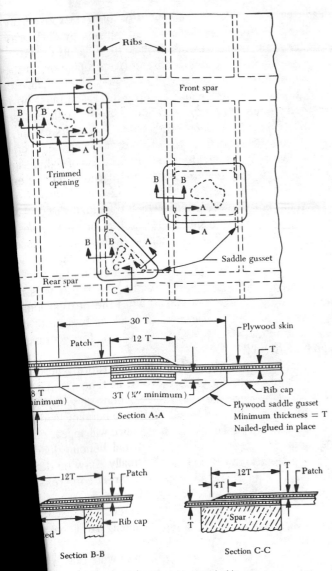

Section A-A

Section B-B

Section C-C

Surface patches on plywood skin.

g the hole. In cases of elongated bolt holes in a spar or
vicinity of bolt holes, a new section of spar must be
e spar replaced. Edge damage, cracks, or other local
ar usually can be repaired by removing the damaged
ing in a properly fitted block, reinforcing the joint by
ood or spruce blocks glued into place.

as a material for framing airplane wings. They insist that spruce wings* are not only as strong as metal-framed ones, but lighter and more flexible. They say the only reason that almost all commercial plane makers have long since switched to metal is simply because wood wings must be hand-crafted, while components of metal wings may be stamped out like doughnuts. These guys concede that wood is subject to deterioration from moisture, and that glue and varnish must be renewed after so many years—while reminding you that metal corrodes and rusts, can suffer from fatigue, and that such airframes must also be refurbished after so many years. Wood, they say, will last as long as metal if it's properly maintained; and nostalgia aside, there are enough Fairchild 24s, Aeronca Chiefs, and Beech Staggerwings still flying to prove it.

"Properly maintained" is clearly the operative term in this contention. And since it is axiomatic that readers aren't interested in writers' opinions (just the facts, man), we'll spare you ours on this question while getting to the nitty part of the gritty on wood inspection.

Dry rot and wood decay are not usually hard to detect. Dry rot shows up as small patches of crumbling wood. A dark discoloration of the wood surface or gray stains running along the grain are indicative of water penetration. If such discoloration can't be removed by light scraping, the part must be replaced. Local staining of the wood by the

---

*Other woods acceptable for aircraft use are: Doublas Fir, Noble Fir, Western Hemlock, Northern White Pine, Port Oxford White Cedar, and Yellow Poplar. But check with you nearest General Aviation District Office before repairing or replacing any wood structure with any type wood except that which was used by the manufacturer.

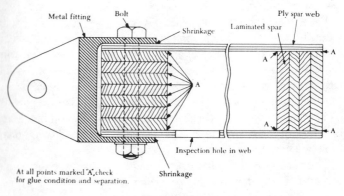

At all points marked "A", check for glue condition and separation.

Laminated wooden joint.

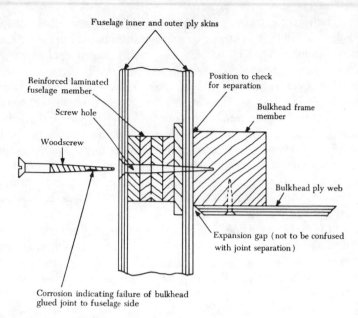

Checking a wooden joint for water penetration.

Labels in figure:
Fuselage inner and outer ply skins
Reinforced laminated fuselage member
Screw hole
Woodscrew
Position to check for separation
Bulkhead frame member
Bulkhead ply web
Expansion gap (not to be confused with joint separation)
Corrosion indicating failure of bulkhead glued joint to fuselage side

dye from a synthetic hardener (used in some bonding agents) may be disregarded.

In some instances where water penetration is suspected, the removal of a few screws from the area in question will reveal, by their degree of corrosion, the condition of the surrounding joint.

The adhesive used will cause slight corrosion of the screw following the original construction; but if the screw is compared with similar screws taken from other parts of the structure known to be free of water soakage, then its condition tells the story.

Plain brass screws are normally used for reinforcing glued wooden members, although zinc-coated brass is sometimes used. For hardwoods such as mahogany or ash, steel screws are sometimes used. It's usual to replace screws with new ones of the same length but one gauge larger.

Another means of detecting water penetration is to remove the bolts holding the fittings at spar root-end joints, aileron hinge brackets, etc. Corrosion on the surface of these bolts and wood discoloration will constitute bad news.

The condition of the fabric covering on ply surfaces is of great importance. If any doubt exists regarding its protective qualities, or if there are any signs of poor adhesion, cracks, or other damage, it

should be removed and the condition of the
examined. Water penetration will be shown
along the grain and a dark discoloration at ply jo
these marks can't be removed by light scrap
advanced deterioration, where there are sr
separation of the ply laminations, the plyw
Where evidence of water penetration is foun
ply surface should be uncovered to determ

During the inspection, you will of cours
bent metal fittings, elongated bolt holes, sig
fuel tanks, and the general condition of t
includes even dust, because dust is a coll

Where bolts secure fittings which take
or where the bolts are subject to landing
holes should be carefully examined for elor
of the wood fibers. Remove the bolts for
sure that the bolts fit well in the holes
aircraft-grade hardware. Some shade-t
known to employ bolts purchased from

Check for evidence of damage suc
structural members which can be cau
tightening of bolts.

Compression failures are caused
fibers. This is a serious defect which
Special care is necessary when insp
which has been subjected to an exces
sion load during a hard landing. Any fa
of a member subjected to an abno
surface subjected to tension will no
case of a member taking an excessi
failure will usually be apparent on

If a compression failure is sus
the member, with the beam of light
help in revealing this type of failu

A lot of the older, low-hp light
ribs and spruce spars. Perhaps
inspecting the spars are damage f
ration of the protective varnish
and/or cracked metal fittings (wi
compression damage. Actually,
have been relatively trouble-fre

All bolts and bushings used
into the holes. Looseness allow

forth, enlargi
cracks in the
spliced in or t
damage to a s
section and g
means of ply

CHAPTER 8
SPARK PLUGS

Well, my fellow aeronauts, when it comes to avoiding lead deposits on spark plugs, we can offer two diametrically opposed recommendations; one from the FAA, and one from the makers of Champion spark plugs. The FAA says (*A&P Mechanics Powerplant Handbook*, EA-AC 65-12), "Lead fouling may occur at any power setting, but perhaps the power setting most conducive to lead fouling is cruising with lean mixtures." And the Champion people say, "The use of economy cruise leaning wherever possible will keep deposits to a minimum."

This is a mite confusing until you sort out the "qualifiers." The FAA is assuming that you are burning the fuel in your engine that it was designed for; and that being so, their statement is correct.

Champion, however, released their recommendation in 1976 (*Sport Flying* magazine; Volume 10, No. 4), when 80 octane av gas almost disappeared from the U.S. market, and Champion was thinking in terms of 100 octane fuel in 80 octane powerplants.

Anyway, Champion is also correct, because lead-fouling of spark plugs is primarily rooted in cylinder-head and oil temperatures. Burning the proper fuel, a lean mixture at cruise power leaves cylinder and oil temps relatively low. But try the same thing with 100LL Blue or 100 Green in your tanks and an engine designed for 80 octane. Yep, she runs significantly hotter. So, the key is a 175 to 200-degree F oil temp. Maintain this at cruise power and the spark plug lead deposits should be minimal. Go ahead and lean the mixture; but do so with an eye on the oil temperature gauge.

Single-piece cowl on the Cessna 152 gives quick and easy access to spark plugs—and almost everything else.

This probably won't solve all your problems burning 100 octane in an 80 octane engine (as this is written, 80 octane is generally available again; but there's no guarantee that it will remain so). Since 100 octane av-gas contains a great deal more anti-knock tetraethyl lead (TEL) than 80 octane, your engine oil may quickly accumulate excessive amounts of lead which, when carried to the high temperature areas of the engine, will cause other problems such as sticking values. The only remedy for this is strict observance of a 50-hour oil drain period. If exhaust valves are sticking, it'll probably be necessary to ream the valve guides and go to a 25-hour oil-change interval.

There are a couple of other things that you can do whenever possible, regardless of the kind of fuel you are using. Avoid both fast let-downs that over-cool the engine and prolonged ground operation.

Now, assuming that you burn the fuel in your engine that it is rated for, you can still get lead deposits if the fuel contains TEL no matter what the octane. And if lead fouling is detected (or suspected) before the spark plugs become completely fouled, the lead can normally be eliminated or reduced by either a sharp rise or a sharp decrease in combustion temperature. This imposes a thermal shock on cylinder parts, causing them to expand or contract. Since there is a different rate of expansion between the lead deposits and the metal

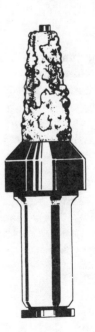

Lead-fouled spark plug.

Carbon-fouled spark plug.

parts on which they form, the deposits chip off or are loosened and then scavenged from the combustion chamber by the exhaust, or are burned in the combustion process.

Several methods of producing thermal shock to cylinder parts are used. The method used, of course, depends upon the accessory equipment installed on the engine. A sharp rise in combustion temperatures can be obtained on all engines by operating them at full take-off power for about one minute. When using this method to eliminate fouling, the propeller control must be place in low pitch (high rpm) and the throttle advanced slowly to produce take-off rpm and manifold pressure. Slow movement of the throttle provides reasonable freedom from backfiring in the affected cylinders during the application of power.

Another method of producing thermal shock is the use of excessively rich fuel/air mixtures. This method suddenly cools the combustion chamber because the excess fuel does not contribute to combustion; instead, it absorbs heat from the combustion area. Some carburetor installations use two-position manual mixture controls, which give a lean mixture setting for cruising economy and a richer mixture setting for all powers above cruising. Neither setting on this type will produce an excessively rich fuel/air mixture. Therefore, to get a richer mixture than the carburetor is capable of

delivering, the primer system is used to add to the normal fuel flow.*
Enrichment and thermal shock can be effected by the primer at all
engine speeds, but its effectiveness in removing lead decreases as
fuel metering through the normal channels increases. The reason for
this is that all electric primers deliver a nearly constant fuel flow at all
engine speeds and powers in a like period of time. Therefore,
comparatively speaking, the primer will enrich the lean mixtures of
low engine speeds far more than it would the richer mixtures that go
with higher engine speeds.

Regardless of the power setting at which primer purging is
used, the primer should be used continuously for a two-minute
period. If normal engine operation is not restored after a two-minute
interval, it may be necessary to repeat the process several times.
Some priming systems prime only the top cylinders; in which case,
only those cylinders receiving the priming charge will be purged.

Graphite Fouling of Spark Plugs

As a result of careless and excessive application of thread
lubricant to the spark plug, the lubricant will flow over the electrodes
and cause shorting. The graphite in the lubricant is a good electrical
conductor. Use care when applying this lubricant to make certain
that smeared fingers, rags, or brushes do not contact the electrodes
or any part of the ignition system except the spark plug threads.
There is no way to burn off this stuff in flight.

Spark Plug Gap Erosion

Spark plug electrodes erode as the spark jumps the airgap
between them. As the gap is enlarged with erosion, the resistance
that the spark must overcome in jumping the airgap also increases.
This means that the magneto has to produce higher voltage; and with
higher voltages in the ignition system a greater tendency exists for
the spark to discharge at some weak insulation point in the ignition
harness. Since the resistance of an airgap also increases as the
pressure in the engine cylinder increases, a double danger exists at
take-off and during sudden acceleration with enlarged airgaps. Insulation breakdown, premature flashover, and carbon tracking result in
misfiring of the spark plug, and go hand-in-hand with excessive
spark plug gap. Wide gap settings also raise the "coming in speed" of
a magneto and therefore cause hard starting.

---

*Electric primers only.

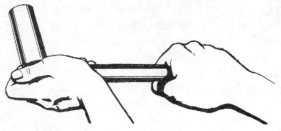

Proper technique for spark plug removal.

Spark Plug Removal

Spark plugs should be removed for inspection and servicing at the intervals recommended by the manufacturer, or if fouling problems have been encountered. Since the rate of gap erosion varies with different operating conditions, engine models, and type of spark plug, engine malfunction traceable to faulty plugs may occur before the normal servicing time is reached. As mentioned earlier, this is particularly true if you've been burning 100 octane fuel with a high TEL content in an engine designed for 80 octane av-gas.

Careful handling of the spark plugs during removal and installation can't be overemphasized. Aircraft spark plugs are easily damaged. The plugs should always be handled individually. If a plug is dropped on the floor or other hard surface, it must not be installed in the engine until pressure-tested, because the impact usually causes small, invisible cracks in the insulators.

Before a spark plug can be removed, the ignition harness lead must be disconnected. Using the special elbow wrench, loosen and remove the spark plug-to-elbow coupling nut. Take care to pull the lead straight out; if a side-load is applied you'll damage the barrel insulator and lead terminal. If the lead can't be easily removed, the neoprene collar may be stuck to the shielding barrel. Break it loose by twisting the collar as if it were a nut being unscrewed from a bolt.

After the lead is disconnected, select the proper size deep socket for plug removal. Apply a steady pressure with one hand on the hinge handle, holding the socket in alignment with the other hand. Failure to hold the socket in correct alignment will result in damage to the spark plug. If carbon deposits have penetrated the lower threads of the spark plug shell, a lot of pressure may be needed to break the spark plug loose.

Service Tips Prior to Installation

Before installing new or reconditioned spark plugs, the bushings or Heli-Coil inserts in the cylinder heads should be cleaned.

Brass or stainless steel bushings are usually cleaned with a spark plug bushing cleanout tap. Before inserting the tap in the hole, fill the flutes of the tap (channels between threads) with clean grease to prevent hard carbon or other material removed by the tap from dropping into the cylinder. Align the tap with the bushing threads by sight were possible, and start the tap *by hand* until there is no possibility of the tap cross-threading the bushing. If the plug hole is too deep to reach by hand, use a short piece of hose slipped over the square end of the tap to act as an extension.

When screwing the tap into the bushing, be sure that the full tap cutting thread reaches the bottom thread of the bushing. This will remove carbon deposits from the bushing threads without removing bushing metal. If, during the thread-cleaning process, the bushing is found to be loose in the cylinder, cross-threaded, or otherwise seriously damaged, the cylinder will have to be replaced.

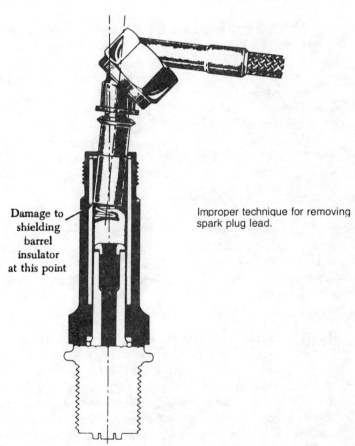

Damage to shielding barrel insulator at this point

Improper technique for removing spark plug lead.

Spark plug Heli-Coil inserts are cleaned with a round wire brush, preferably one having a diameter slightly larger than the diameter of the spark plug hole. A brush considerably larger may cause removal of material from the Heli-Coil proper or from the cylinder head surrounding the insert. Also, the brush should not disintegrate with use, allowing wire bristles to fall into the cylinder. Clean the insert by carefully rotating the wire brush with a power tool. When using the power brush, be careful not to remove material from the spark plug gasket seating surface, because this can cause a change in the spark plug's heat range, combustion leakage, and eventual cylinder damage. *Never* clean the Heli-Coil inserts with a cleaning tap because permanent damage to the insert will result. Damaged Heli-Coil inserts must be replaced.

Using a lint-free rag and cleaning solvent, wipe the gasket seating surface; and before installing new plugs inspect each for the following:

1. Make sure the plug is the approved type for your engine.
2. Check for evidence of rust-preventive compound on the plug's exterior, core insulator, and inside the shielding barrel. If necessary, wash the plug in solvent and dry with an air blast.
3. Check both ends of the plug for nicked or cracked threads and any indication of cracks in the nose insulator.
4. Inspect the inside of the shielding barrel for cracks in the barrel insulator, and the center electrode contact for rust.
5. Check the spark plug gasket; if excessively flattened or distorted, replace.

The gap setting should be checked with a round wire thickness gauge. A flat-type gauge will not give you a correct reading because the ground electrodes are contoured to the shape of the round center electrode. Insert the gauge in each gap and center it. The proper airgap clearance will be specified by the plug manufacturer.

Spark Plug Installation

Begin by thoroughly stirring the anti-seize compound that goes on the first two or three threads of the spark plug, and be very careful not to get any of it on the electrodes or the nose of the plug.

Installing the spark plug, screw it into the cylinder with your fingers until it seats on the gasket. Then, only small additional torquing is needed to get a gas-tight seal. If there are dirty or damaged threads on the plug or plug bushing, quite a bit of torque

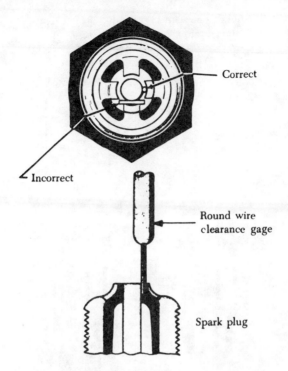

Correct

Incorrect

Round wire
clearance gage

Spark plug

Use of the gap-measuring gauge.

may be needed and this usually turns it into a task of by guess and by God. Too much torque may compress the gasket out of shape and stretch the plug shell. Shell stretching occurs as excessive torque continues to screw the lower end of the shell into the cylinder after the upper end has been stopped by the gasket shoulder. This breaks the seal between the core insulator and shell. But if the bushing and plug threads are clean and undamaged, you can screw the plug down to the gasket with your fingers and then use a torque wrench to tighten to the specified torque value.

Spark Plug Lead Installation

Before attaching the spark plug lead, clean the terminal sleeve (often called the "cigarette") and the integral seal with a cloth moistened with acetone, MEK, or an approved solvent, then inspect it for cracks and scratches. Damaged and heavily stained terminal sleeves should be replaced.

Next, slip the lead into the shielding barrel of the plug and tighten the coupling elbow nut with the proper tool. "Proper" in this

87

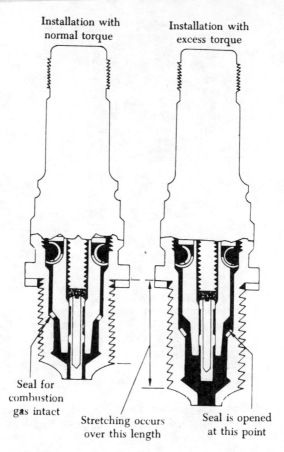

Installation with normal torque

Installation with excess torque

Seal for combustion gas intact

Stretching occurs over this length

Seal is opened at this point

Effect of excessive torque in installing a spark plug.

case being a 3/4 or 7/8-inch end wrench, preferably one that has been sawed in half to make it harder to over-torque the elbow nut, and easier to work with in the restricted space. There really is a special tool for this; but nobody ever has one.

CHAPTER 9
AIRCRAFT BATTERIES

The lead-acid storage batteries used in airplanes are basically the same as those used in automobiles. The voltage is determined by the number of cells connected in series. A lead-acid cell, regardless of the number and size of the plates it contains, produces two volts. So, a battery rated at 12 volts has six cells connected in series, and a 24 volt battery has 12 cells.

The capacity of such batteries is rated in ampere-hours (amperes furnished by the battery times the amount of time current can be drawn). This rating indicates how the battery may be used at a given rate before it becomes completely discharged.

The ampere-hour capacity of a battery depends upon its total effective plate area. Increase the number of plates per cell, and you increase the ampere-hour capacity. Or, connect two or more batteries in parallel and you get the same effect. The voltage remains the same.

Connect batteries in series to increase voltage. Connect batteries in parallel to increase capacity. (Larger airplanes usually use two or more batteries connected in parallel.)

In theory, a 100 ampere-hour battery will furnish 100 amperes for one hour; 50 amperes for two hours; etc. Actually, the ampere-hour output depends upon the rate of discharge, and under service conditions the battery can be completely discharged within a few minutes, or it may never go down if the generator or alternator provides sufficient charge.

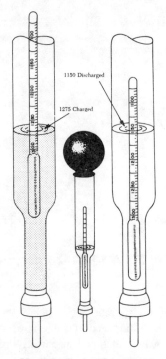

1150 Discharged

1275 Charged

Battery hydrometer. A simpler type
employs three colored balls.

Various factors cause deterioration of a battery and shorten its
service life. These include over-discharging (which causes excess
sulfation, internal heating, and shedding of active material). A battery that remains in a low or discharged condition for a long period of
time may be permanently damaged.

The state of charge of a battery is indicated by the density of the
electrolyte, and is checked by a hydrometer, a simple device that
measures the specific gravity weight of liquids as compared with
water.

The hydrometer allows you to draw a sample of the electrolyte
into its glass tube where the float will show the fluid's specific
gravity. In a fully charged battery, the electrolyte is approximately
30 percent acid and 70 percent water (by volume) and is 1.300 times
as heavy as pure water. During discharge, the electrolyte becomes
less dense and its specific gravity drops. Therefore, a specific
gravity reading between 1.275 and 1.300 reveals a high state of
charge. Readings between 1.240 and 1.275 indicate a medium
charge, and anything below that a low charge. An aircraft battery in a
low state of charge may have as much as 50% of its charge remaining, but you have to regard it as marginal because of heavy demands
that may be placed on it.

Care must be taken when making a hydrometer test of a lead-acid cell, because the electrolyte contains sulfuric acid which will burn clothing and skin. If this acid should contact the skin, the area should be washed thoroughly with water and then bicarbonate of soda applied.

The battery box in lightplanes has a removable top, with a vent-tube nipple at each end. One tube is the intake and is exposed to the slipstream. The other is the exhaust and is attached to the battery drain sump, a glass jar containing a felt pad moistened with a concentrated solution of bicarbonate of soda (baking soda). This set-up neutralizes battery gases and carries them outside the airplane, but is not found on all light aircraft.

Perhaps it should be, because, when charging rates are excessive, the electrolyte can boil to the extent that fumes containing droplets of the electrolyte are emitted through the cell vents. These fumes from lead-acid batteries may become noxious to crew members and passengers. Some kind of battery vent system is necessary to prevent this explosive mixture from accumulating.

Electrolyte spillage or leakage can cause serious corrosion of the nearby structure or control cables. It may be spilled during ground servicing, leaked when cell case rupture occurs, or sprayed

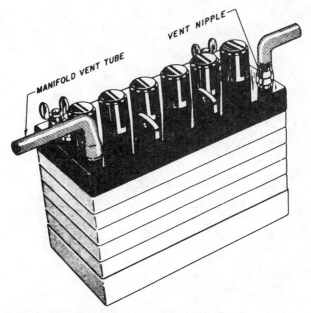

Aircraft battery with integral vent nipples.

from cell vents due to excessive charging rates. If your battery is not enclosed, nearby structural parts must be properly treated to protect them from acid fumes.

To prevent freeze damage to a lead-acid battery you must maintain the specific gravity (charge) to a reasonably high level, bearing in mind that such batteries are subject to a constant discharge due to the internal chemical action. A fully charged lead-acid battery will freeze at minus 95 degrees F (−70 C); but when its specific gravity drops to 1.150 it will freeze at + 5 degrees F (− 15 C), and fully discharged it may freeze at + 20 degrees F (− 8 C).

Battery Installation

1. Clean the external surfaces of the battery prior to installation.
2. When replacing lead-acid batteries with nickel-cadmium batteries, neutralize the battery box or compartment and thoroughly flush with clear water and dry. Acid residue is damaging to the ni-cads.
3. Check condition of the vent system.
4. Exercise care to prevent inadvertent shorting of the terminals. Serious damage to the aircraft structure can result if both terminals come in contact with any part of the airframe simultaneously.
5. Battery holddown devices should be secure, but not so tight that they damage the battery.

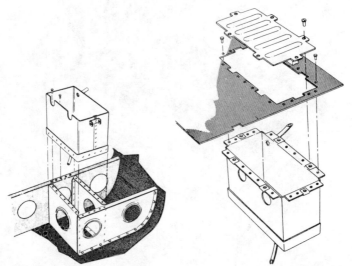

Typical battery box installations. Aft fuselage location (L), and suspended from cabin floorboard section at right.

Nickel-Cadmium Batteries

The increasing use of the nickel-cadmium aircraft battery stems largely from its low maintenance cost derived from its long service life. It also has a short recharge time, excellent reliability, and good starting capability.

The electrolyte in the ni-cad is a 30 percent solution (by weight) of potassium hydroxide (KOH) in distilled water. Its specific gravity remains between 1.240 and 1.300 at normal temperatures, and no appreciable changes occur in the electrolyte during charge or discharge. For this reason, the battery charge can't be measured by a specific gravity check of the electrolyte.

The ni-cad battery is usually interchangeable with the lead-acid type. If you are switching to a ni-cad from a lead-acid battery, thoroughly clean the battery compartment and paint it with an alkali-resisting varnish. The pad in the battery sump jar should be saturated with a three percent (by weight) solution of boric acid and water before connecting the battery vent system.

The potassium hydroxide electrolyte in the ni-cad is very corrosive; in case it is spilled on clothing or skin, rinse at once with water or vinegar, lemon juice, or a boric acid solution.

When cleaning the battery, the vent plugs should be closed, and no acids, solvents, or chemical solutions should be used. Severe arcing can result if a wire brush is used to clean a battery. Use a fiber brush to loosen any particles (crystals) of potassium carbonate that may form from overcharging, and wipe off the battery with a damp cloth.

Since both the specific gravity of the electrolyte and the voltage of a ni-cad remain fairly constant, about the only way you can test its state-of-charge is to remove it, connect it to a constant-voltage (not constant-current) battery charger, and note the amount of current it draws. The higher the state-of-charge, the smaller the current drawn.

CHAPTER 10
TIPS AND TIE-DOWNS

You should have learned to properly tie down an aircraft while a student pilot. In case you didn't, we'll picture the two knots most commonly used for tie-down; and mention that tie-down anchors for light aircraft should provide a minimum holding power of approximately 3,000 lbs each; that stake-driven anchors may pull out of the ground during a heavy rain; that manila rope shrinks when wet and must be at least one-half inch in size; nylon and Dacron twist rope is best (3/8-in); and that rope should never be tied to a lift strut.

Aircraft Cleaning

Cleanliness not only promotes Godliness, as the old saying goes, but in the case of airplanes, safety as well. A cracked landing gear fitting, covered with mud or grease, is easily overlooked. Dirt can hide cracks in the skin. Dust and grit impose excessive wear on hinge fittings; and a film of dirt on the airplane's outer surfaces reduces flying speed and adds extra weight. Dirt and trash bouncing around the inside of the cabin can be dangerous. Salt water, of course, is highly corrosive on exposed metal parts of the airplane, and should be washed off immediately.

There are three methods of cleaning the aircraft exterior: 1) Wet wash, 2) dry wash, and 3) polishing. Wet wash, using a water-emulsion or alkaline cleaning agent such as XOFF-310, removes oil, grease, carbon deposits, and most soils, except corrosion and oxide films. The cleaning agent is usually applied by spray or mop, after which high-pressure running water is used as a rinse.

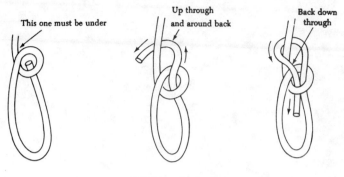

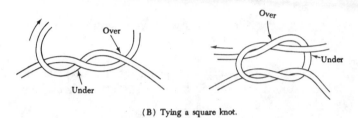

(A) Tying a bowline knot.

(B) Tying a square knot.

Knots commonly used for aircraft tie-down.

Dry wash is used to remove airport film, dust, and small accumulations of dirt and soil when the use of liquids is impractical or undesirable. Dry-wash materials may be sprayed, mopped, or wiped on the surfaces, and removed by dry mopping or wiping with clean, dry cloths. They will not remove heavy deposits of carbon, grease, or oil, especially around the engine exhaust.

Polishing restores luster to painted and unpainted surfaces following a good cleaning. It is also effective against oxidation and corrosion.

Diagram of recommended tie-down dimensions.

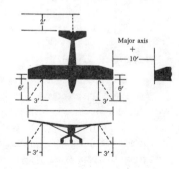

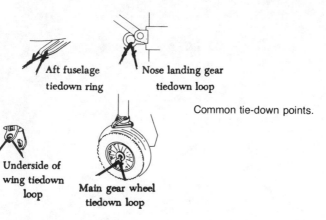

Aft fuselage
tiedown ring

Nose landing gear
tiedown loop

Common tie-down points.

Underside of
wing tiedown
loop

Main gear wheel
tiedown loop

Whenever possible, always wash your aircraft in the shade, because most cleaners tend to streak the paint when applied to hot surfaces. The cowl top finished with a dull paint should not be cleaned more than necessary, and should not be scrubbed with stiff brushes or coarse rags. And any oil or exhaust stains should be taken off with solvent and rinsed immediately.

A mild soap solution is best for removing oil, hydraulic fluid, grease, or fuel from aircraft tires.

After cleaning, lubricate all grease fittings, hinges, etc., where removal, contamination, or dilution of the grease is suspected during washing of the aircraft.

Unfortunately, not all A&Ps will leave the airplane's cabin as clean as it should be following service/repair work. Use a vacuum cleaner to pick up any metal particles or other debris as soon as possible. Any nuts, bolts, bits of wire, or other metal objects carelessly dropped and neglected, combined with moisture and dissimilar-metal contact, may cause electrolytic corrosion. Dust and other lighter particles could get into your eyes during flight at a critical time and prove very dangerous.

The care of windshields and windows is discussed in Chapter 6, so we'll not repeat that here.

Powerplant Cleaning

A clean engine is important because grease and dirt accumulations provide an effective insulation against the cooling air flowing over it. Such accumulations also hide such things as cracked engine mounts and other possible trouble spots.

When cleaning the engine, open or remove the cowling. Then, starting at the top, wash down the engine and accessories with a fine

96

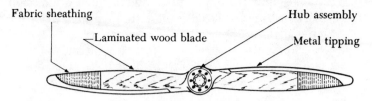

Fabric sheathing Hub assembly

Laminated wood blade Metal tipping

Fixed-pitch wooden propeller

spray of solvent (kerosene is still used for this, but it isn't our favorite cleaner). A bristle brush may be used to help clean some of the surfaces.

Caustic cleaners should not be used on the propeller, nor should scrapers, power buffers, steel brushes, or any tool or substances that will mar or scratch the aluminum-alloy blades. In flight, water spray, rain, and other airborne abrasive particles strike the blades with such force that small pits are formed in the blades' leading edges. It is permissible to smooth these out with #00 sandpaper or crocus cloth. However, the exact extent to which the pilot/owner may legally go in removing metal from his propeller constitutes one of those gray areas in the FARs (in this case, 35.31). To be on the safe side, both legally and physically, always consult your A&P before doing anything to your propeller besides washing it with a mild soap and water.

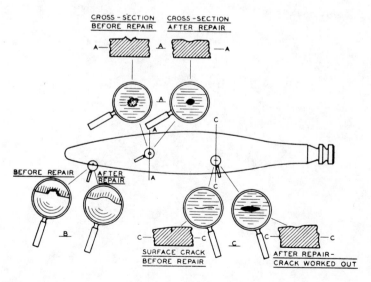

Method of repairing surface cracks and nicks on aluminum alloy propellers.

After cleaning the powerplant, all control arms, bell-cranks, and moving parts should be lubricated according to instructions offered in your airplane's maintenance manual.

If your airplane is equipped with a wooden propeller, you should periodically check to make sure that the drain holes in the tips are open, and that the safety wire on the hub-bolts is secure.

Mechanical Cleaning Materials

Powdered pumice is used for cleaning corroded aluminum surfaces. Similar mild abrasives may also be used.

Impregnated cotton wadding material is used for removal of exhaust-gas stains and polishing corroded aluminum surfaces. It may also be used on other metal surfaces to produce a high reflectance.

Aluminum metal polish is used to produce a high luster, long-lasting polish on unpainted aluminum. It should not be used on anodized surfaces because it will remove the oxide coat.

Three grades of aluminum wool, coarse, medium, and fine, are used for general cleaning of aluminum surfaces. Impregnated nylon webbing material is preferred over aluminum wool for the removal of

Fixed-pitch aluminum installed on Stinson Voyager.

corrosion and stubborn paint films, and for scuffing of existing paint prior to touch-up.

Lacquer rubbing compound material can be used to remove engine exhaust stains and minor oxidation. Heavy rubbing over rivet heads or edges where protective coatings may be worn thin should be avoided.

Abrasive papers used on aircraft surfaces should not contain sharp or needlelike abrasives that can imbed themselves in the base metal being cleaned or in the protective coating being maintained. Aluminum oxide paper, 300 grit or finer, is available in several forms and is safe to use on most surfaces. The use of carborundum (silicon carbide) papers should be avoided, especially on aluminum and magnesium, because individual grains will penetrate, bury themselves even in steel surfaces, and promote corrosion. The use of emery paper and crocus cloth can also cause serious corrosion by imbedding iron oxide in the surface.

Chemical Cleaners

Chemical cleaners must be used with great care in cleaning assembled aircraft. The danger of entrapping corrosive materials in faying surfaces and crevices outweighs any advantages in their speed and effectiveness. Any materials used must be relatively neutral and easy to remove. We should emphasize that all residue must be removed. Soluble salts from chemical surface treatments such as chromic acid or dichromate treatment will liquefy and promote blistering in the paint coatings.

A phosphoric-citric acid mixture (Type I) for cleaning aluminum surfaces is available and is ready to use as packaged. There is also a Type II, which is a concentrate and must be mixed with mineral spirits and water. When applying, you should wear rubber gloves and a face shield or goggles. Any acid burns may be neutralized by copious water washing, followed by treatment with a diluted solution of baking soda.

CHAPTER 11

INSPECTION PROCEDURES

The most effective way to insure that your airplane is maintained in top condition is to establish a continuous inspection schedule. Develop a system of inspection and an inspection checklist that includes the complete aircraft, and once adopted, don't deviate from it.

Such a system will give priority to key safety items, and the engine and flight control system; and in setting up this program take into account climatic conditions, frequency and type of flying you do, contemplated periods of inactivity, and the kind of storage facilities you have.

After you have determined inspection intervals for the powerplant and flight control system, you can decide on the periods for the rest of the aircraft components. A good method is to establish your inspection intervals on the basis of flying hours. If your flying is done over the weekends, you may find it handier to inspect one or more items each weekend. In any case, spread your inspection program over a period of time that is reasonable from a safety standpoint and does not make unreasonable demands on your time. Here are examples recommended by the FAA:

By Hours

Daily preflight inspection.
Powerplant (including propeller and engine controls), every 25 hours.
Flight control system, every 25 hours.
Fabric, every 75 hours.
Landing gear, every 50 hours.
Cabin/cockpit, every 100 hours.

By calendar weeks

Daily preflight inspection.

Powerplant and flight control system, first weekend.

Landing gear, third weekend.

Powerplant and flight control system, fourth weekend.

Cabin/cockpit, fifth weekend.

Fabric, sixth weekend.

Powerplant and flight control system, seventh weekend.

You may find it convenient to establish a combination of both methods; but regardless of the method you adopt, adhere to it faithfully.

To maintain your airplane's Airworthiness Certificate, the FARs require that your craft must have a periodic inspection during the preceding 12 calendar months and approved for return to service by a certificated mechanic holding an inspector's rating, an FAA certified repair station, or manufacturer authorized to conduct such inspections. This is commonly referred to as the "annual inspection," and it includes a certain amount of servicing. Your mechanic will work from an extensive check list and give you a copy showing the operations performed.

Both the periodic and the 100-hour inspections are complete inspections of the aircraft, identical in scope. The periodic must be performed by an A&P with an inspector's rating (only an AI has the authority to return a plane to service), while any certified rated mechanic may perform the 100-hour inspection. This is why the periodic will take the place of the 100-hour inspection while the reverse is not true.

Oxidation

Oxidation is caused by the chemical union of metal and oxygen in a damp atmosphere. We usually refer to oxidation as "rusting" when speaking of steel or iron parts. The oxidation of copper, aluminum, dural, and other similar metals is usually called "corrosion." The appearance of rust is well known to everyone, but you should know that it can be present where it can't be seen. Steel tube members of an aircraft equipped with floats must always be suspect. It's possible for water to enter the interior of this tubing, allowing rust to form on the *inside* while the exterior appears to be in good condition. The best way to check for this condition is to drill small holes in the bottom of the tubing while the airplane is in level attitude. If water is present, it will run out the holes. Such a test should be performed by (or under the supervision of) your A&P. He'll know where and how to drill the tubing—and how to restore the area tested. If time, usage, or structural repair requires that the steel tubing in your fuselage receive renewed internal rust protection (the tubing interior was treated when the airplane was built), a preservative oil meeting MIL Spec L-21260 such as the Stits Tubeseal, will recoat the tubing's interior. Tubeseal will also seep through and reveal any tiny pinholes in welded joints and, in time, congeal and reseal them.

Corrosion

Corrosion of aluminum surfaces is usually caused by damage to or deterioration of the metal's protective coating. Corrosion can also be caused by the paint coming in contact with battery acid, insecticide spray, etc. Contact between two dissimilar metals is still another cause of corrosion, as is exposure to salt water.

Corrosion appears as white or grayish-white powder or flakes. If pitting of the metal is apparent after cleaning off the flakes or powder film, an experienced mechanic should be consulted for his assessment of the damage. On aluminum surfaces that have been painted, watch for paint bubbles or blisters. Corrosion can take place under the paint; therefore, the suspected part should be cleaned to the bare metal and examined in the blistered area.

Fuselage Inspection

1. Open or remove all inspection plates, access doors, and fairings. Take note of any oil or other foreign accumulation that indicates fluid leakage or other abnormal condition, then clean all fittings such as landing gear and wing strut attachments. Inspect the structure with a magnifying glass, looking for cracks, poor welds, and elongated bolt holes. Check the structural tubing or bulkheads for signs of distortion, cracks, loose bolts and rivets. Determine that the structure is free from rust and corrosion.

2. Inspect the fabric or metal skin for tears, distortion, deterioration, and other defects. Loose rivets may be spotted by a dark "collar" of oxidation working from beneath the rivet head. Remember that fabric on the upper surfaces usually deteriorates first—but this doesn't lessen the need to check the airplane's belly, which can be damaged by rocks thrown back by the wheels or propeller-wash, or damaged from the inside by, say, battery electrolyte.

3. Check external bracing and attachment fittings for distortion, cracks, and rust. Inspect the adjustable ends of brace wires for cracks, excessive bearing wear, damaged threads, and loose locking nuts. Wing struts may be damaged by stepping on them when entering or leaving the airplane, or by mishandling on the ground. Generally speaking, it's better to replace a bent lift strut rather than attempt repair.
4. Examine the control system's bellcranks for cracks, misalignment, and security of attachment. Check cables for proper tension and routing through fairleads and pulleys. Rotate pulleys to check for flat spots, to provide new bearing surfaces for the cables, and to check for smooth, free operation. Inspect hydraulic lines for leaks and chafing.
5. Check the electrical wiring for proper installation and security of attachment. Inspect the rubber grommets, any plastic tubing, and the electrical connectors. Wiring that has been damaged as a result of chafing should be replaced.
6. Inspect fuel tanks and filler caps for proper alignment, security of attachment, and evidence of leaks. Make sure that the vents and vent lines are free of obstructions. Examine the fuel lines and connections for leaks, cracks, security of attachment, and chafing. Make sure that the overflow and drain lines are not kinked or broken, and that they extend beyond the aircraft structure.

Fuel systems include either a fuel tank sump and/or a sediment bowl (gascolator) to trap water and sediment. Periodically drain a

FLIGHT CONTROLS

sufficient amount (at least 10 ounces) of fuel from the tank sumps, if installed. It is normal to drain the gascolator as part of your pre-flight or "walk-around" inspection prior to each day's flying. Some modern lightplanes incorporate a system that allows you to perform this operation from the pilot's seat. While this makes it easy, it does deny you the chance to see how much, if any, contamination is present.

7. Inspect cabin doors for general condition, ease of operation, and security of attachment. Determine that the doors can be positively locked to prevent inadvertent opening during flight.

Cabin/Cockput Inspection

1. Inspect the cabin for loose articles that might interfere with control operation. Using a flashlight, inspect under the instrument panel for loose wires and leaks in the instrument lines.
2. Check the fuel selector valve(s) for leaks, freedom of movement, and determine that it positions properly at each setting. Check the fuel gauges for accuracy. Check the engine primer for leaks and satisfactory operation.
3. Inspect the electric wire bundles for chafing and security of attachment. Examine the connections at terminals, junction boxes, cannon plugs, and check clips for looseness. Check condition of circuit breakers, fuses, and switches.
4. Check hydraulic fluid level. Inspect hydraulic bypass and relief valves for leaks. Trace hydraulic lines, checking for leaks, dents, kinks, cracks, and chafing. *Never* mix dissimilar hydraulic fluids.
5. Inspect all instruments for security of attachment. Check bulbs in panel warning lights. Inspect instrument panel shock mounts. A period check of vacuum operated instruments is recommended to prevent erratic operation due to dirty filters. Dirty filters, of course, must be replaced.
6. Inspect all control linkage for proper functioning. Check cables for frayed strands and proper tension. Examine pulleys and fairleads for misalignment, breakage, or looseness. Inspect bellcranks and torque tubes for alignment, cracks, freedom of movement, and proper safetying. Determine that the pulleys and fairleads through which the control cables pass are clean, and that the surrounding

structure in no way interferes with their movement. Operate the controls to make sure that there is no lost motion, binding, or chafing.

7. Inspect seats for security of attachment and proper functioning of the adjustment mechanism. Examine safety belts and shoulder harnesses. Make sure that the latching devices are in good condition, and that the attachments to the airframe are sound.

8. Make certain the hand-operated fire extinguisher is fully charged and secure in its mounting.

9. Check condition of the cabin heating and ventilating system. Look for leaks and examine lines and fittings.

10. Inspect all windows and the windshield for cracks, discoloration, cleanliness, and freedom of operation.

Engine Inspection

Now, some of the procedures that follow are recommended in the FAA Advisory Circular AC 20-9 which is, according to its preface, "intended primarily for use by student mechanics, pilots, and especially personal aircraft owners." This reporter suggests that one follow a simple rule here: Anytime you take apart and reassemble anything under the engine cowling, do so under the watchful eye of a licensed A&P. True, a gascolator, for example, is a very simple device; and the cleaning of carburetor screens should be properly accomplished by anyone who is capable of tying his own shoe laces. Still, it's probably best to touch base with your A&P before cleaning and inspecting such components for the first time.

Now, we realize that a lot of pilots use a different rule, that one being that it's legal (or at least practical) for them to perform, unsupervised, any maintenance operation that doesn't have to be entered in the engine log. Who's going to know the difference? Well, clearly, the FARs can't say it that way because, human nature being what it is, such a rule would soon be stretched to absurd (and unsafe) lengths. Again, there's no substitute for common sense. Now let's get on with the engine inspection:

1. Remove, clean, and inspect the gascolator or main fuel strainer screens. Check for water and dirt contamination. Inspect the bale wire bearing surfaces for excessive wear.

When reassembling the gascolator, be careful in tightening the bale wire. If it isn't tight enough, the bowl will leak, while too much pressure can chip or break the bowl. Be sure that trapped air is eliminated to assure unrestricted fuel flow.

With fuel selector and boost pump on, inspect the fuel lines and their connections for leaks, cracks, kinks, chafing, and security of attachment. Examine hoses and clamps for tightness and general condition. Make sure that the fuel lines do not interfere with adjacent equipment or lines.

Examine the primer system and perform an operational check. Make sure that all connections are tight and that soldered joints have not separated. Copper primer lines must be annealed periodically (by your A&P) to relieve brittleness.

Inspect the carburetor for security of attachment, leaks due to damaged gaskets, and for loose or damaged fuel line fittings. Look for excessive wear at the throttle shaft, link assemblies, and hot air butterfly shaft bearing points, any one of which can affect the fuel-air mixture resulting in erratic engine operation. Drain the carburetor bowl and examine the gasoline for signs of water or other contaminants. Remove and clean carburetor screens. Flush the carburetor by turning on the fuel supply momentarily. Replace screens, drain plugs, and re-safety.

Remove and clean the carburetor air filter.

Make sure that the carburetor heater is properly secured, and that heater doors operate throughout their full range.

Examine the intake manifold for cracks, kinks, and evidence of leakage. Make sure that the upper and lower packing nuts are tight and not leaking. If rubber hose is used, inspect for condition and security of its clamps. A small amount of gasoline, applied at intake manifold joints and connections with squirt can, will reveal leaks, because it will be drawn into the intake and cause a brief surge of rpms when the engine is idling. If leaks around the packing nut can't be corrected by tightening the nut, the packing gland will have to be replaced.

2. If yours is a dry sump engine, inspect the oil tank for evidence of cracks or oil leaks, especially around the welded seams and at fittings. Also check the tank for chafing at the adjustable retainer straps, and for security of attachment. When changing oil, strain it through a screen or cloth in order to check for foreign particles, particularly bits of metal that may indicate internal engine damage.

Inspect the oil lines for leakage and security of attachment, particularly at connections.

On wet sump engines, remove sump plug and inspect for foreign particles. Remove, inspect, and clean oil sump strainers. Reinstall drain plugs and strainers and safety immediately.

If your lubrication system incorporates an oil radiator, examine it for leaks and security of attachment.

3. Determine that the magneto holddown nuts are tight and properly safetied. Inspect magneto cover screws for security and tightness. If the holddown nuts are found to be excessively loose, it'll be necessary to check the magneto timing to make sure that it has not been altered.

Examine the ignition wiring and connections for general condition. Inspect spark plug barrels, elbows, and knurled nuts for proper tightness and alignment. Check the magneto ground wires for proper attachment to the terminal and ignition switch. Remember, if a magneto is not properly grounded, it is possible for the engine to start, even though the magneto switch is in the OFF position. So, NEVER trust a propeller at rest, especially when the engine is warm.

4. Inspect each exhaust stack for condition and security of attachment. Check that no portion of the engine cowling has been in contact with or is wearing on the exhaust system. Make sure that all support bolts are tight and safetied.

5. Inspect the engine cylinders for cracked or broken fins. Check the baffles for security, holes, cracks, and proper fit around the cylinders. Inspect all air entrances and exits for deformations that might obstruct the airflow. Using a flashlight, look through the nose cowling and check for gaps between the top cowling and engine baffles.

Since most air-cooled engines require pressurized air for cooling, any leak around or through the baffles causes a pressure drop and therefore reduces the cooling efficiency of the engine.

If your airplane is equipped with cowl flaps, make sure that they are in good condition; that hinges are not excessively worn, and that the actuating mechanism is properly rigged for full travel and is operating properly.

You know, of course, that operation of the cowl flap(s) is of vital importance in keeping cylinder head temperatures within the required operating range.

6. Remove the heater shroud from the exhaust manifold and inspect the manifold for cracks, burned-out spots, or defective welds. Determine that shut-off valves are operating through their full travel; cold air and heater ducts are free of obstructions and cracks, and are properly secured. If

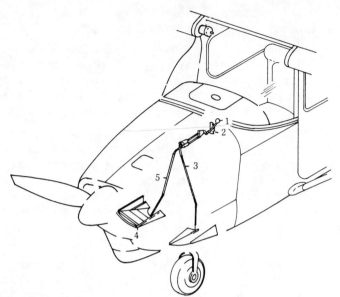

1. Cowl flap control lever   2. Position bracket   3. L.H. cowl flap control

4. Cowl flaps   5. R. H. cowl flap control

Lightplane cowl flap system.

your heater incorporates an intensifier tube in the manifold, it should be removed and inspected for cracks and burned-out spots.

Defects in the heater system must be repaired immediately to insure that carbon monoxide or flames will not enter the cabin.

7. Using a magnifying glass, examine the engine mount structure, especially at welds, for evidence of cracks. Make sure that all attachment bolts are tight and properly safetied.

8. Examine the mounting of all accessories, such as the generator or alternator, starter, oil pump, oil pressure relief valve body, etc., for security of attachment, oil leakage, and proper safetying.

9. Inspect the engine cowling for defects such as cracks, dents, chafing on portions of the engine or airframe, loose rivets, clamps, and fasteners. The presence of dark streaks on aluminum structure usually indicates chafing caused by vibration and looseness.

10. Check the condition of the firewall behind the engine, and inspect the insulation for oil or fuel saturation, which condition presents a serious fire hazard.

11. Check the battery box and terminals for corrosion and security. Inspect the vents and overflow lines for obstructions and proper routing. Examine the battery electrolyte level and, using a hydrometer, determine the charge of the battery. If the hydrometer test shows a variance of more than 20 points between cells the battery should be recharged or replaced. If the electrolyte level is low, add distilled water. The airplane will have to be flown for at least 30 minutes after adding battery water before the electrolyte can be accurately tested.

It's good practice to protect the area adjacent to the battery with an acid-proof paint. When working around the battery, care should be taken to avoid short-circuiting across the terminals as the resultant arcing creates a serious fire danger. As a safety precaution, the battery should be removed during cleaning and repair operations, removing the "ground" terminal first.

Landing Gear Inspection

1. Inspect the tires for proper inflation; look for cuts, bulges, and foreign objects embedded in the tread. Excessive wear may be caused by misalignment of the wheels, scissors assembly, or axles. Under-inflation promotes sidewall cracks, while over-inflation results in abnormal crown wear. Unbalanced wheels cause uneven tire wear and vibration which can in turn damage other parts of the aircraft.

Some tires have a color tracer or color thread imbedded in the carcass. When the tire wears enough to reveal this tracer it's time to recap or replace it. In any case, replace the tire when the tread wears smooth. It's poor economy to make a few bucks by stretching tire life while risking damage to your airplane.

Gasoline can cause rapid deterioration of rubber in a tire. Don't allow oil or gasoline to drip on tires, and don't park your airplane in an accumulation of gasoline or oil.

2. Jack up the airplane, remove the wheel, and inspect the brake assembly for broken or distorted parts, broken springs, and worn lining. Faulty or missing spring clips may cause the brakes to chatter. Check the condition of the

discs, expanders, or shoes according to which of these types you have. Examine the brakes for security of nuts, bolts, and cotter pins. Determine that the foot and parking brake controls are in good condition, operating properly, and are safetied. Any defects found in your braking system should be referred to your A&P for repair.

If you have mechanical brakes, check the cables for fraying. Inspect the pulleys for ease of turning, alignment, and broken attachments. Check the actuating arms for proper bearing and throw. Check the brake pedals for proper operation.

If your brakes are hydraulically activated, inspect the fluid lines for damage or obvious defects. Check the system for leakage around wheel, master cylinders, and all connections. Inspect for deterioration and security of flexible tubing. Check fluid level in the reservoir. A low fluid level may indicate a leak somewhere in the system, requiring a more thorough inspection of the system. Always use the type of brake fluid recommended by the manufacturer, and never mix different types. A "spongy" pedal may indicate air in the brake system or other abnormal condition that needs the attention of your mechanic.

3. Inspect the wheels for damage and cracks. A bent or distorted wheel flange usually indicates that it is cracked or broken. Check tightness of wheel bolts. Before reinstalling the wheels, clean and check condition of the wheel bearings and lubricate (see Chapter 2). With the wheel installed on the axle and adjusted, check for excessive side-play by moving the wheel back and forth against the thrust washer and adjusting nut.

4. There are many kinds of shock absorber systems in use on airplane landing gears. Some Mooneys and Beechcrafts employ rubber biscuits in compression; Cessnas use spring steel gear legs; some Rockwell-built craft smooth out the bumps with fiberglass slabs, and many older craft use rubber shock cords a la Piper Cub (and Tri Pacer). Most, perhaps, are equipped with the oleo-type air-oil shock struts.

Generally speaking, the rubber biscuit in compression, and the spring steel shock absorbers require little, if any, maintenance. However, a careful examination of the area where the attachment brackets join the airframe should be made. Inspect for cracks and any sign of rivet or bolt failure.

Where rubber shock cords are employed, inspect for general condition, cleanliness, stretching, and fraying. Shock cords must be kept free from accumulations of gasoline, oil, and mud. As noted earlier in this book, the FARs allow pilot/owners to replace rubber shock cords. It's legal, but not advisable. Too many people have been injured attempting this operation. So, if your plane has rubber shock cords which need replacing, have your A&P do it. He has the tools, experience, and knowhow.

Inspect oleo-type shock absorbers for cleanliness, leaks, cracks, and possible bottoming of the pistons. Check all bearings, bolts, and fittings for condition, lubrication, and proper safetying. Refer to Chapter 2 for procedures to be followed in replenishing fluid and pressure charge.

5. *Fixed landing gear*: Perform a close visual inspection of the main landing gear for cracks in the vicinity of welds. Examine attachment fittings for condition and elongation of bolt holes.

Wrinkled fabric or metal skin detected in the area of the attachment fittings should be called to the attention of your A&P for his analysis.

Inspect struts for cracks, bowing, and security of attachment. Check braces and fittings for general condition.

Excessive play between fittings may be more readily detected if the wheel is off the ground and the landing gear vigorously shaken in a fore and aft direction, as well as up and down. If noticeable clearance is detected at any of the attaching points, the bolts should be removed and inspected for wear and distortion. Defective bolts should be replaced immediately, and distorted bushings and fittings repaired or replaced. Since there will be considerable movement at the bearing surfaces, it is essential that they be inspected carefully and properly lubricated at frequent intervals.

Inspect the nosewheel assembly for general condition and security of attachment. Examine linkage, trusses, and members for evidence of undue wear or distortion. Ensure that all bolts, studs, and nuts are secure with no indication of excessive wear and are properly safetied. If a shimmy damper is installed, make sure that it is operating satisfactorily and the steering mechanism is correctly rigged.

Steerable tailwheels should be inspected for bearing adjustment, lubrication, clearance, and range of operation. Check for proper steering action and security of attachment.

6. *Retractable landing gear*: Particular attention should be paid to locking mechanisms, drag struts, shock struts, stops, linkages and alignment. Be sure the shock strut is properly inflated and the piston is clean and oiled. Examine fairing doors for satisfacory operation, proper rigging, and for loose or broken hinges.

When new or retread tires are installed, a gear retraction test should be performed (with the airplane on jacks) to check for adequate clearance. The wrong tire size can cause the gear to hang up in the well.

Check the nose/tailwheel and main gear-up latches for proper operation of the entire latch assemblies. Inspect the down-lock mechanism and power source for general condition.

Refer to your owner's manual for lubrication instructions.

Inspect the retracting and extending mechanism of the nose or tailwheel and main landing gear for general condition, defects, and security of attachment. Determine that actuating cylinders, sprockets, universals, and chain or drive gears are in good condition and within the manufacturer's tolerances.

If the gear is electrically operated, inspect the motors for security of attachment. Make sure that the wiring is in good condition and properly routed and secured to prevent interference with movable members. Determine that protective rubber or plastic caps are installed over all wire terminals requiring such protection.

Inspect the landing gear warning system microswitches for cleanliness, condition, security of attachment, and proper operation. With the aircraft on jacks, check the landing gear warning horn system with the electrical power ON by retarding throttle with the gear retracted. Check this wiring for routing, freedom from chafing, and general condition.

Water accumulation in microswitches may freeze at altitude, making the switches inoperative. Adjustments to microswitches should be attempted only by an experienced A&P.

If your landing gear is hydraulically operated, inspect all actuators for general condition, leakage, and operation throughout their full range of travel. Determine that lines, reservoirs, accumulators, and valves are securely attached and not leaking. Make sure that the lines are free from chafing and securely attached to the adjacent airframe. Check entire gear operation using normal hydraulic pressure.

7. *Float installations*: Examine the floats for obvious defects and damage to the skin. Check for loose rivets, screws,

nails, and condition of the glue. Inspect the structure for cracks, and drain any accumulation of water from each compartment.

Inspect the float attachment fittings for cracks and defective welds. Examine hinge points for wear. Check the struts and bracing for proper attachment, alignment, and safetying. Due to the rigidity of such an installation, you should make a thorough inspection of the fittings and the adjacent airframe structure where the struts attach to the aircraft.

8. *Ski installations*: The skis should be inspected for obvious damage, security of rigging, and main axle attachment fittings. Special attention should go to the ski pedestal. Periodically inspect the ski bottoms for tears or cracks. If installed, check the hydraulic system for leaks and proper fluid level. Inspect for condition and proper rigging of all devices restraining the skis from tipping downward at their front edges.

Wing Inspection

Determine the condition of the wing and center section by carefully inspecting fixed surfaces for signs of deterioration, distortion, and loose or missing rivets or screws, especially in the area of fabric or skin attachment to the airframe. Inspect the fabric or skin for tears, distortions, or other defects, including corrosion. Inspect the fabric at its juncture with the windshield for deterioration and security of attachment. Review the earlier chapter in this book which deals with fabric problems.

Check the drainage grommets for security of attachment and for obstructions. If yours is a fabric covered airplane that has been re-covered since new, ask yourself (and your A&P) if the grommets are effectively located at *all* low points and places where water might collect inside the wing's trailing edge and ahead of the ailerons.

Remove all fairings, fillets, and inspection plates and open all access doors to inspect the internal wing structure. A flashlight—and often an angled mirror—will be needed here. Check the condition of the spars, ribs, compression members, drag wires, rib lacing or whatever kind of skin attachment is employed. Examine the protective varnish on any wood members, and carefully study any glued joints (see chapter on wood structures). Inspect wire or metal tube bracing for proper tension and for any sign of distortion. Especially check all fittings. Your wing should be clean inside. Any

Numerous and properly positioned drain grommets on underside of top wing on this beautifully restored Beech Staggerwing.

accumulation of dirt (which attracts moisture) or oil or grease should be cleaned away and its source identified.

When inspecting your airplane, it's a good idea to make notes on any condition that leaves you in doubt, and give this list to your A&P when you are finished. Then, follow him around as he re-checks those places and offers his opinions. You'll be surprised at how much you'll learn this way.

Inspect the movable surfaces (ailerons, flaps, and trim tabs) for loose or pulled rivets, distortion, and skin condition. Examine hinges and horns for security of attachment, bends and breaks. Inspect hinges for loose or worn pins, proper lubrication, and safetying. Remember that external distortion may be the result of internal failure.

Since control surface imbalance may cause a dangerous flutter or vibration in flight, any repair or even refinishing of balanced control surfaces must be left to an experienced A&P.

Inspect the external brace fittings (struts or brace wires) where they attach to the wing for distortion, cracks, or other defects. Inspect the clevises for wear, cracks, worn or damaged threads.

If any rigging adjustment of the external bracing has been done on a biplane, particular care should be taken to assure that there is a sufficient number of threads holding in the adjusting terminals. Most terminals are provided with a test hole in the shank. If safety wire can be inserted through the test hole, the required number of threads are not holding in the terminal. Another test is to count the threads on the male fitting. If more than three threads show, the connection is not satisfactory.

Determine that the wing attachment fittings are not distorted, cracked, or damaged in any way, and that the bolt holes have not become elongated. Check the bolts as well for cracks and looseness. You will, of course, thoroughly clean these fittings before inspection, and a magnifying glass is advisable in case hairline cracks are present.

Examine the aileron, flap, and tab controls for proper operation. Inspect bellcranks for cracks, alignment, and security. Check cables for proper tension, fraying, wear, and correct routing through fairleads and pulleys.

2. Inspect the fuel tanks for security of mounting and signs of leakage. Assure that the filler caps are secure and the vent is pointing the right way and free of obstructions. Check the fuel lines and connections for leaks, security of attachment and chafing. Be sure that overflow and drain lines are not kinked or broken and are correctly routed to the outside air. Improperly placed vents and those that are kinked or otherwise distorted can cause fuel starvation and engine failure.

As a precaution against getting the wrong kind of fuel, make sure the placard located at or near the filler neck is legible.

3. Inspect pitot tubes or masts for obstructions, distortion, and security. Make sure that the static ports are clean and free of obstruction. Periodically, you should have your A&P drain and clean out pitot and static lines.

4. Inspect all wiring for chafing, proper routing (especially, secured away from control mechanisms), condition of grommets, plastic tubing, adapters, and proper taping. Inspect landing lights for extension, retraction, and general condition. Also examine the navigation lights for condition and operation.

5. Determine that the hydraulic lines in the wings are free from cracks, kinks, dents, leaks, and wear due to chafing. Assure that the hydraulic actuators are securely mounted and not leaking.

Empennage Inspection

Inspect the fixed tail surfaces for loose rivets, screws or bolts, cracked fittings, and condition of covering and drain grommets. Examine the condition of ribs and stabilizer spars at points of attachment for cracks and elongated bolt holes.

1. Movable control surfaces, such as elevators, rudder, and trim tabs, should be examined for distortion, loose rivets, fabric or skin defects, and condition of drain grommets. Inspect hinges and horns for security of attachment, breaks or bends. Examine hinges for loose or worn pins, proper lubrication, and safetying. If your airplane is equipped with a stabilator instead of elevators, its key attachment and control components are accessible for inspection either via an access door or plate at the rear of the fuselage, or by removal of the tail cone.

2. Examine the fabric or metal skin for damage, especially on the bottom surfaces, which can take a beating if your craft has been operated off unimproved fields.

3. Inspect the external bracing attachment fittings for distortion, cracks, and security of attachment. Check struts or brace wires for condition and security of attachment. Examine clevises for cracks, worn or damaged threads, and any other apparent or obvious defects.

Bracing must not be slack, which could cause flutter, nor should there be excessive tension, which can distort or damage the fittings, pull the surface out-of-rig, and place undue stress on the structure. If you are in doubt concerning any aspect of the external bracing, put it on your list as one of the things you will consult with your A&P about.

4. Inspect the control cables and bolts for wear at horns or bellcranks; look for such things as frayed or chafed cables, pulleys not turning, misplaced cable guides, rusty or corroded tubing, and broken welds. Inspect the trim adjustment mechanism for excessive looseness, security of attachment, and proper operation of the trim adjustment position indicator. If the aircraft is trimmed by either an adjustable stabilizer or trim tab, they must operate freely throughout their designed range of travel. (The Piper Cubs sometimes developed restricted travel of the stabilizer, and this led to some interesting landing procedures.) Lubricate as required; but never over-lubricate because oil and grease attract dust.

5. Inspect the navigation lights for condition and operation. Check wiring for chafing, proper routing, and security of attachment. Check the routing grommets, plastic tubing, adapters, and for proper taping.
6. Inspect the gust locks for condition. Assure that they release completely and cannot possibly engage inadvertently.

Propeller Inspection

If any unsatisfactory conditions are found while inspecting your propeller, your A&P should be consulted for a determination whether repairs or replacements are necessary. All propeller repairs, other than a few minor ones, must be done by either the manufacturer or a propeller repair station. Hubs should be lubricated as recommended by the manufacturer, using lubricants listed in your aircraft owner's manual.

A propeller blade should never be used as a handhold for moving an airplane. It is extremely easy to impose forces on a blade in excess of those for which the blade was designed.

1. Inspect metal blades completely for corrosion, cracks, nicks, and scratches, particularly on the leading edge of

Check propeller for nicks, dents, and scratches, especially from tips inward about eight inches along the leading edges.

each blade from the tip inboard for approximately eight inches. Nicks and scratches set up concentrations of stress which can exceed the strength of the blade material; the result will be a crack leading to blade failure.

Wood or composition blades should be inspected for condition of metal tipping and leading-edge strips. Check for loose rivets or screws, separation of soldered joints, and other signs of creeping and looseness of the metal tipping. Check for lamination separation, especially between the metal leading edge and cap, and for condition of fabric sheathing. Inspect the tips for cracks by grasping with your hand and slightly twisting and bending the tip backward and fore-ward. A fine line appearing in the plastic or fabric will indicate a crack in the wood. Assure that tip drain holes are open. These must be kept free of obstructions so that the centrifugal force of the revolving propeller will force out excess moisture. If yours is other than a fixed-pitch propeller, make certain that the blades are installed in the hub satisfactorily and properly safetied. The wood close to the metal sleeve of wood blades should be examined frequently for cracks extending outward on the blade.

2. Inspect the hub for corrosion, cracks, oil leaks, security of attachment, and correct safetying. Assure that the propeller retainer bolts are tight and properly safetied.

3. Inspect the propeller control system for security of attachment, oil leaks, and freedom of movement. Inspect the wiring for condition, routing, and chafing. Inspect the tubing for security, kinks, scratches, oil leaks, and chafing. Assure that all exposed nuts are tight and properly safetied.

The control system may incorporate a full-feathering mode including relays, solenoids, governors or control valves, and distributors. Inspect the various external components of the system for security of attachment, oil leaks, chafing, or obvious damage to the electrical wiring. Check for loose connections and proper safetying. We should note that certain engine-prop combinations require that a spinner be installed to facilitate proper engine cooling. In such cases, the engine should not be operated unless the spinner is in place.

4. If installed, inspect the propeller spinner and spinner mounting plate for security of attachment, cracks, chafing of the blades, and apparent or obvious defects, along with correct safetying. Cracked spinner assemblies must be removed and repaired immediately by your qualified A&P to prevent the possibility of parts breaking away from the

spinner in flight and seriously damaging portions of the aircraft structure, or injury to personnel while operating on the ground.

5. If installed, inspect the anti-icer assembly for general condition and security. Assure that the slinger ring, nuts, and delivery tubes are correctly installed and that the nuts holding the delivery tubes to the slinger ring sockets are securely fastened. Inspect the fluid level, and reservoir and lines for proper installation, chafing and leakage. Check the connections for condition and security of the clamps.

Radio Inspection

1. Inspect electrical wiring and shielding for defects, chafing, and security; assure that connections, terminals, and clips are tight. Look for evidence of shock-mounted equipment contacting adjacent components or structure. Check the fuses for corrosion, condition and security.

Periodically, radio equipment should be removed to inspect shock mounts and bonding, and to clean and inspect racks and adjacent structure. Plugs and connectors should be opened and inspected for corrosion, dirt, and moisture. Assure that all plugs and connectors are properly mated and secured. *Caution*: Disconnect the battery ground cable before removing radio equipment.

As a rule, no serious consequences other than poor reception will result from broken bonding strips. But since good radio reception is important to the safe operation of your airplane, broken bonding strips should be immediately replaced.

2. Examine installation of communication and navigation equipment (radio, ADF, OMNI, DME, etc.) for security of attachment. Check all jacks, knobs, and switches for security. Volume controls should work smoothly. Switches should have positive action. Indicator dials should be clean and have proper motion. Check for defective light bulbs. Spare light bulbs and fuses should be readily available in the cabin.

Headsets and microphones should be inspected for broken or sticking switches, dirty, worn, or damaged plugs. Inspect the cord for excessive wear or other damage.

If a portable radio is used, some means of securing the unit should be provided in the aircraft to keep it in place during turbulence in flight.

Open the junction boxes and inspect for extraneous material, security of connections, and condition of wiring and cables. Inspect remote control shafts for condition, security, and ease of operation.

3. Check the antennas for condition and security of attachment. Inspect wire antennas for proper tension. Inspect insulators, fittings, terminals, and supporting masts for condition and security. Clean all insulators. A broken antenna may foul the controls or cause other serious damage. Inspect rigid antennas and masts for evidence of lightning strikes. Check the rubber seals for evidence of cracks or leakage.

4. Check the manual and automatic rotation of the loop. Remember, when refinishing the airplane, the loop housing requires a special kind of paint.

5. Inspect the power supply installation for security of attachment. Check the wiring and connections for proper grounding, condition, insulation, and security. Check the switches for operation and security. Also, periodically check the dynamotors for security of attachment and cleanliness.

6. Inspect the static trailing wicks for proper length, condition, and security.

An operational check should be performed on all radio equipment during engine warm-up. Reception should be free of interference caused by ignition, generators/alternators, navigation lights, strobes, or any other electrical or mechanical unit. Unsatisfactory operation of communication or navigation equipment should be referred to a licensed aircraft radio repair shop.

CHAPTER 12

THE PRE-FLIGHT INSPECTION

Your "walk around" or pre-flight inspection, performed prior to the first flight of the day, is a more or less standardized ritual. The following checklist may be applied to almost any single-engine or light twin-engine airplane, provided that it is modified wherever necessary to conform with the manufacturer's recommendations on any given airplane.

Before Entering the Airplane

1. Cockpit/Cabin:
   Battery and ignition switches—"OFF."
   Control locks—"REMOVE."
   Landing gear switch—"DOWN."
2. Fuselage; Right Side:
   Baggage compartment—contents secure and door locked.
   Airspeed static source—free of obstructions.
   Condition of fabric/metal skin—generally eyeball for damage, distortion, missing rivets, cracks, tears, etc.
   Anti-collision and nav lights—condition and security.
3. Empennage:
   Control surface locks—"REMOVE."
   Fixed and movable control surfaces—dents, cracks, excess play, hinge pins and bolts for security and condition.
   Tailwheel—spring, steering arms and chains, tire inflation, and condition.

The pre-flight inspection takes only a few minutes, and is one of the safety habits that separates the old pilots from the bold pilots. (There are no old, bold pilots.)

Lights—navigation and anti-collision lights for condition and security.

4. Fuselage; Left Side:
Same as item Two.

5. Wing; Left side:
Control surface locks—"REMOVE."
Control surfaces, including flaps—dents, cracks, excess play, hinge pins and bolts for security and condition.
General condition of wings and covering—torn fabric, bulges or wrinkles; loose or missing rivets, etc.
Wing tip and nav light—security and damage.
Landing light—condition, cleanliness, and security.
Stall warning vane—freedom of movement. Prior to inspection turn master switch "ON" so that warning signal is checked when the vane is deflected.

6. Landing gear; Left side:
Wheels and brakes —condition and security; indications of fluid leakage at fittings, fluid lines and adjacent area.
Tires—cuts, bruises, excessive wear, and proper inflation.

Oleos and shock struts—cleanliness and proper inflation.

Shock cords—general condition.

Wheel fairings—general condition and security. On streamline wheel fairings, look inside for accumulation of mud and ice.

Limit and position switches—security and cleanliness.

Ground safety locks—"REMOVE."

7. Fuel tank; Left side:

Fuel quantity and proper grade (color).

Filler cap and fairing covers—secure.

Fuel tank vents—obstructions.

If your fuel tank is equipped with a quick, or snap-type drain valve, drain a sufficient amount of fuel into a container (a glass jar is best) to check for water and sediment.

8. Engine:

Engine oil quantity—secure filler cap.

General condition and evidence of fuel and oil leaks.

Cowling, access doors, and cowl flaps—condition and security.

Carburetor filter—cleanliness and security.

Drain a sufficient quantity of fuel from the main fuel sump drain to determine that there is no water or sediment remaining in the system. Primary source of water in the fuel is condensation from temperature changes, which is why it is advisable to fill your tanks at the end of each day's flying.

9. Nose landing gear:

Wheel and tire—cuts, bruises, excessive wear, proper inflation. Check valve stem for damage.

Oleo and shock strut—proper inflation and cleanliness.

Wheel well and fairing—general condition and security.

Limit and position switches—cleanliness, condition, and security.

Ground safety lock—"REMOVE."

10. Propeller:

Propeller and spinner—security, oil leakage, and condition. Especially look for deep nicks and scratches.

Assure that ground area under the prop is free of loose stones, cinders, etc.

11. Fuel tank; Right wing:

Same as item 7.

12. Landing gear; Right side:

Same as item 6.

Among other things, your pre-flight inspection will include a visual check of each fuel tank (F), oil (O), spinner and propeller (P), shock strut assembly (S), and tires.

    13. Pitot:
        Pitot cover—"REMOVE."
        Pitot and static ports—obstructions, alignment, and general conditon.

    14. Wing; Right side:
        Same as item 5.

After Entering the Airplane

    15. Cockpit / Cabin:
        Check for cleanliness and loose articles.
        Windshield and windows—damage and cleanliness.
        Rudder pedals—adjust so that full travel is assured.
        Safety belt and shoulder harness—condition and security. Fasten.
        Parking brake—"SET."
        Check all switches and controls, including landing gear and flap switches for proper position.
        Trim tabs—"TAKE OFF."
        Pilot's seat—"LOCKED."

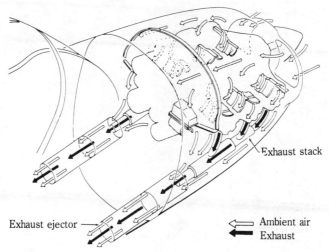

Exhaust stack

Exhaust ejector

⇐ Ambient air
⬅ Exhaust

Most aircraft engines are air pressure cooled and depend upon the airplane's forward speed for proper cooling. To prevent overheating—and spark plug fouling—take-off as soon as possible after the ground run-up is completed.

Ground Run-up and Functional Check

1. It is desirable to have the airplane headed into the wind. Avoid prolonged idling at low rpm, as this may result in fouled spark plugs.
2. Navigation and communication equipment—"OFF."
3. Fuel tank selector valve—to fullest tank.
4. Brakes—"ON."
5. Determine that no one is near your propeller and start engine.
6. Check all instruments for proper operation and indication.
7. Check all powerplant controls. At idle rpm, momentarily switch magnetos to "OFF" to check for proper ground. If the engine should continue to run, that indicates a faulty circuit between the magneto and switch which must be repaired before the airplane is flown.
8. Flight controls—check for free and smooth operation in proper direction.
9. Radio receiver—check and tune to proper frequency.
10. Set altimeter and clock.

125

INDEX